Learning Centers
through the
Year
for Primary Classrooms

Written by Annette Hauenstein Wallace
Edited by Ina Massler Levin
Illustrated by Blanca Apodaca, Cheryl Buhler, Sue Fullam, Keith Vasconcelles, and
Theresa Wright

Teacher Created Materials, Inc.
P.O. Box 1040
Huntington Beach, CA 92647
©*1993 Teacher Created Materials, Inc.*
Made in U.S.A.
ISBN 1-55734-059-5

Table of Contents

Table of Contents *(cont.)*

Introduction

Learning Centers Through the Year for Primary Classrooms is an ideal resource for establishing learning centers in your classroom. It provides all the directions and patterns necessary to set up ten learning centers for every month of the school year—September through June. These 100 activities will keep children actively and enthusiastically involved in independent learning activities.

What Is A Learning Center?

A learning center is an area in a classroom where one or more children can participate in activities designed for enrichment and review of current learning, and for reinforcement of the skills being taught. A learning center coordinated with the curriculum enhances those skills and learning.

A center can consist of games, activities, manipulatives, or reading materials. A listening center with special equipment such as a tape recorder with headphones, a computer, calculator, or typewriter may constitute a center. As new topics are introduced or areas of special interest develop, new centers may be created. Rather than serve as primary instruction, a learning center supports what is taught in the classroom. A center provides an alternative to the traditional concept of seatwork. It allows the student an opportunity to independently practice skills and assume responsibility for learning, while freeing the teacher to work with small groups or individual students.

A learning center should not serve as a place where children can merely spend their "free" time. A successful center has a clearly stated task or objective for each activity. Children should have the opportunity to use the centers daily.

Why Should I Use Learning Centers?

Children learn best when they are actively involved in learning. Manipulating math materials, writing and publishing their own stories, creating plays, exploring the world through maps and globes, or reviewing new vocabulary words are just a few of the learning center activities that get students involved, hands-on. Centers accommodate different learning styles which, in turn, give students an opportunity to become more involved in their own education. As children become more self-motivated, they strengthen their self-esteem. Since many center activities have no right or wrong answers, student creativity abounds.

Learning centers also help children learn how to work independently. As students want to find the answers for themselves, they become more responsible for completing tasks, checking them, and cleaning up. As patterns for using the centers are established, organizational skills develop.

The nature of the learning center gives students freedom to learn on their own. They begin to think more critically and solve problems. Specific activities may require higher levels of thinking, as well as providing an environment that is conducive to this kind of learning.

Introduction *(cont.)*

How Do I Set Up A Learning Center?

The organization and set-up of learning centers are keys to developing a successful program in your classroom. Where and how you place your centers is important, remembering that they must be useable within your classroom. They may be set up on walls, in corners, behind partitions, on tables, on desks, or even in storage bins. Consider storage before arranging the room because centers must be accessible to students. Some centers may require an arrangement of equipment and materials where there is a water source, electrical outlet, or a special light. Wall space around the room is usually a good place to set up learning centers. With such an arrangement children are spread out around the room so crowding doesn't take place. Flexibility is your most important asset in setting up centers.

How Do I Use A Learning Center?

Your first job is to introduce the learning center to the students. Let them know what the centers are for, and how to use and take care of them, including cleaning up. This should be repeated every time new centers are introduced. Plan to spend some time at the beginning of each month explaining the proper procedures to follow at the centers. Tell children what is expected of them. It may be helpful to post procedures and rules near each center. Some general rules include:

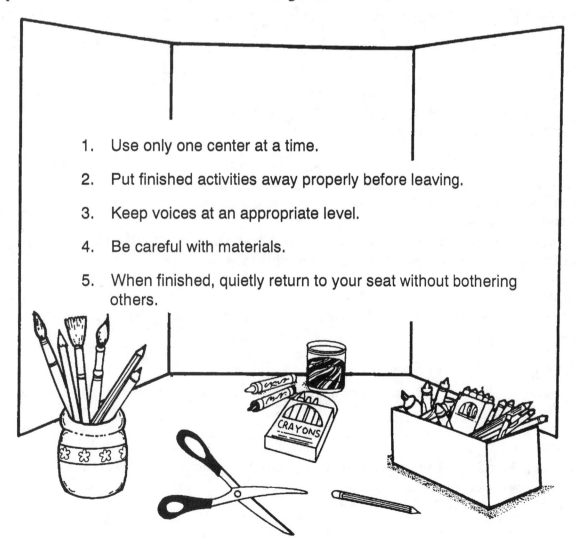

1. Use only one center at a time.

2. Put finished activities away properly before leaving.

3. Keep voices at an appropriate level.

4. Be careful with materials.

5. When finished, quietly return to your seat without bothering others.

Introduction *(cont.)*

What Learning Centers Should I Use?

Learning Centers Through the Year makes it a snap to set up ten learning centers in your classroom. One hundred center activities are included in this book. For each month of the school year you have ten centers:

Reading
Here, students have the opportunity to reinforce reading readiness, reading skills, and enjoy some of their favorite stories.

Games and Puzzles
At this center your students play games that reinforce skills, allow students to challenge each other to games, and have fun completing various types of puzzles.

Math
Students learn math skills using a variety of techniques emphasizing manipulatives.

Science
Students find an opportunity to question and experiment using hands-on activities at the science center.

Seasonal Special
A highlight of the month or season allows your students to research or create a project appropriate to the time of year when they work at this center.

Art
Many opportunities to explore various mediums are available when children enjoy art as a creative outlet.

Drama and Stories
Giving children a chance to express themselves orally through several types of activities are available here, as are stories children can both enjoy and learn from.

Social Studies
Finding out more about the world we live in, the people in our communities, and how we get along highlight this center.

Writing
Expressing oneself through writing, including various forms of poetry and narrative, are among the activities found here.

Hands-On
Getting to experience the manipulation of many different materials allows for student growth in several areas of development.

Introduction *(cont.)*

How Do I Manage Learning Centers?

How do you know which student belongs at which center? Develop some classroom management systems. See the center management section beginning on page 356 for some ideas.

Schedule a time each day for your learning centers. Only you will know how much time in your classroom day to devote to centers. However, ten to twenty minutes is usually ample time for completion of a center, but this may vary. A rotation system may work well for you; have some children working at centers and others working with you. The important thing is to keep track of the centers children have completed.

Make your learning centers look inviting. Decorate them, put up pictures or colorful signs to identify them. Use the materials in this book. They are all reproducible and should be assembled prior to setting up the centers. Durable materials are the best; whenever possible, use heavy paper and laminate. Remember, the materials will be used over and over again and must be strong enough to withstand normal use and handling by students

How Will My Students Benefit From Learning Centers?

The enthusiasm for and results of using learning centers is well worth the time and effort required to set them up. They offer an avenue for reaching each child. Learning centers can play an important part in the daily schedule for primary children. Your children will learn by doing, and enjoy learning while it is taking place.

Beginning Sounds

Purpose
Given beginning sounds, the student can identify pictures that begin with those sounds.

Materials
- 6 large manilla envelopes
- Baseball Billy
- Laughing Lucy
- Dancing Dolly
- Spaghetti Sammy
- Noisy Nettie
- Mighty Mike
- Pictures on pages 15-20

Preparation
Reproduce, color, and cut out the pictures of Baseball Billy Boy, Laughing Lucy, Dancing Dolly, Silly Sammy, Noisy Nettie, and Mighty Mike on pages 9-14.   Glue one each onto a manilla envelope. Cut out the pictures that begin with B, L, D, S, N, and M.

Instructions
Children play only one game at a time. Have them find the pictures that begin with the sound they are looking for. Have them place those that begin with B in the envelope with Baseball Billy, L with Laughing Lucy, D with Dancing Dolly, S with Spaghetti Sammy, N with Noisy Nettie, and M with Mighty Mike.

Clean-Up
Put all game parts in the correct envelope.

8

Baseball Billy

Laughing Lucy

Dancing Dolly

Spaghetti Sammy

12

Noisy Nettie

Mighty Mike

B Words

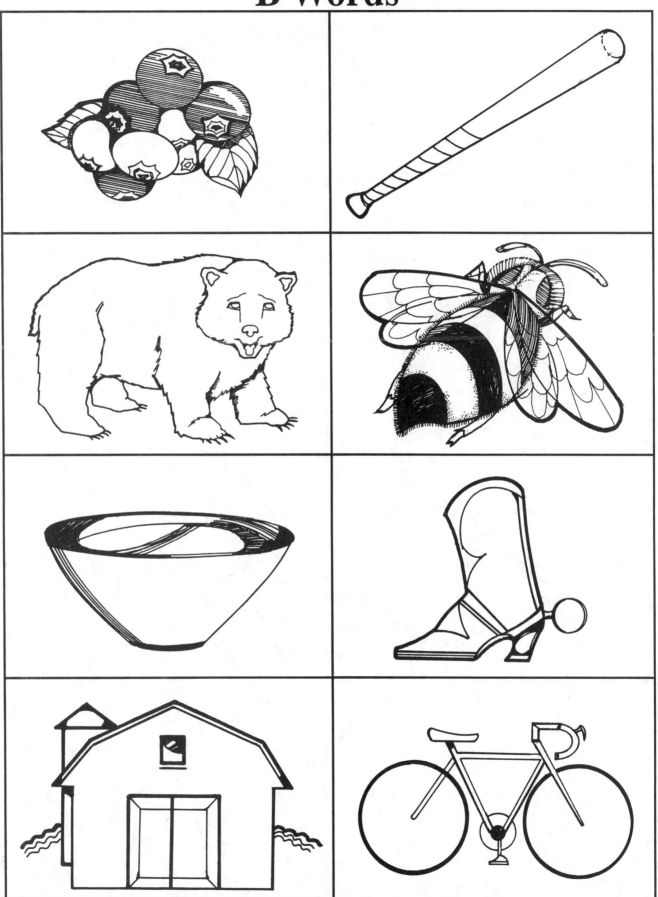

L Words

D Words

S Words

N Words

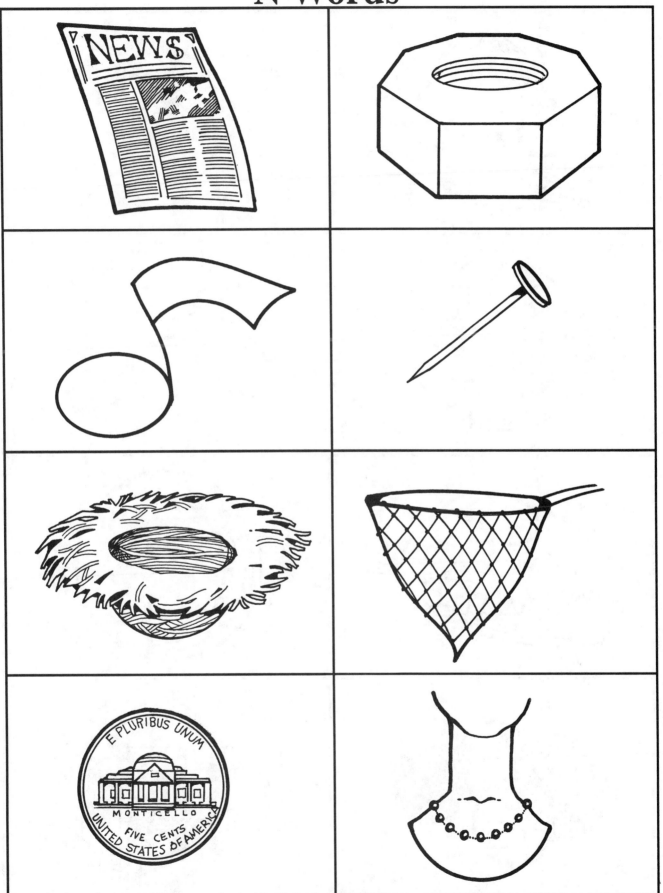

M Words

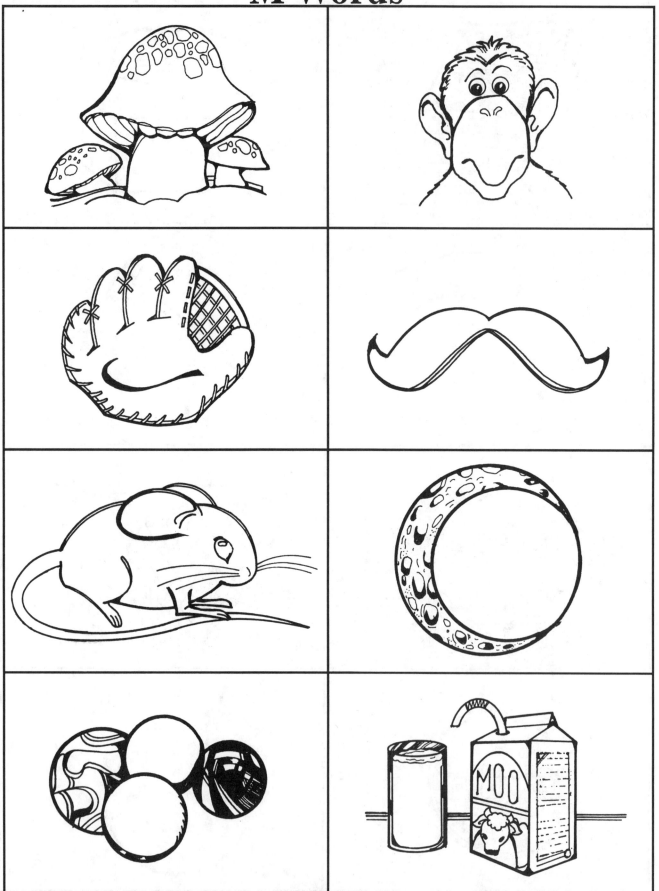

Alphabet Train Puzzle

Purpose

Children review their ABCs as they manipulate the parts of this game. It also helps children make a connection between a picture and a beginning sound.

Materials

- Alphabet train (pages 22-48)
- Manila envelope or file folder for game parts

Preparation

Reproduce onto colored index paper the alphabet train. Cut out and laminate each piece of the puzzle.

Instructions

Have children take the game folder to the floor so there is enough space to put the train together. Start the train with the engine car and then proceed to line up the cars A-Z. Check the children as they complete the alphabet train.

Clean-Up

After completion, store all pieces of the train in the folder or storage envelope.

Helpful Hints

The patterns for the train can be adapted for use as a bulletin board. Reproduce, cut out, and create a classroom display.

Alphabet Train Puzzle *(cont.)*

Engine

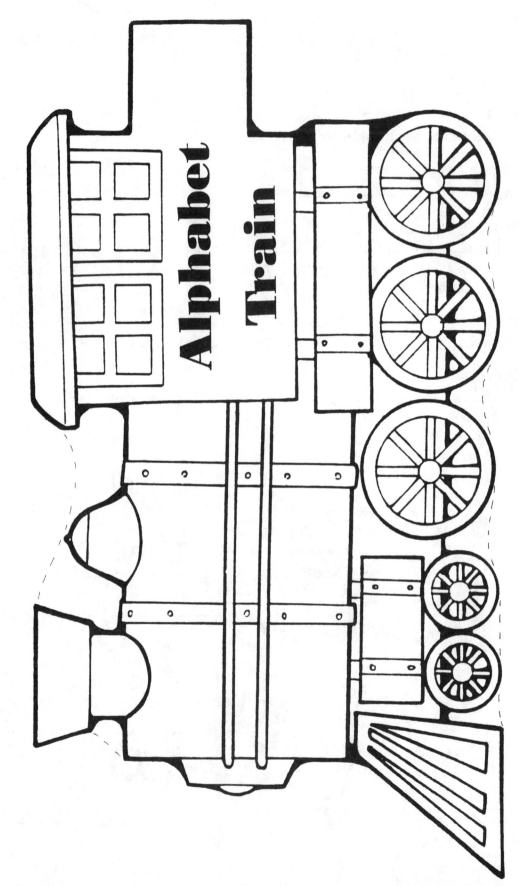

Alphabet Train Puzzle (cont.)

Alphabet Train Puzzle (cont.)

Alphabet Train Puzzle (cont.)

Alphabet Train Puzzle *(cont.)*

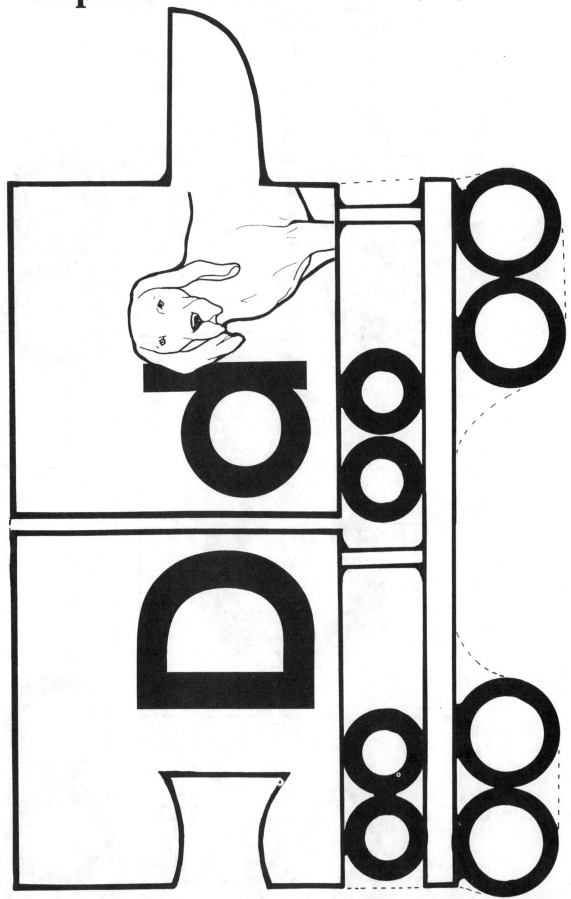

Alphabet Train Puzzle (cont.)

Alphabet Train Puzzle (cont.)

Alphabet Train Puzzle (cont.)

Alphabet Train Puzzle *(cont.)*

Alphabet Train Puzzle (cont.)

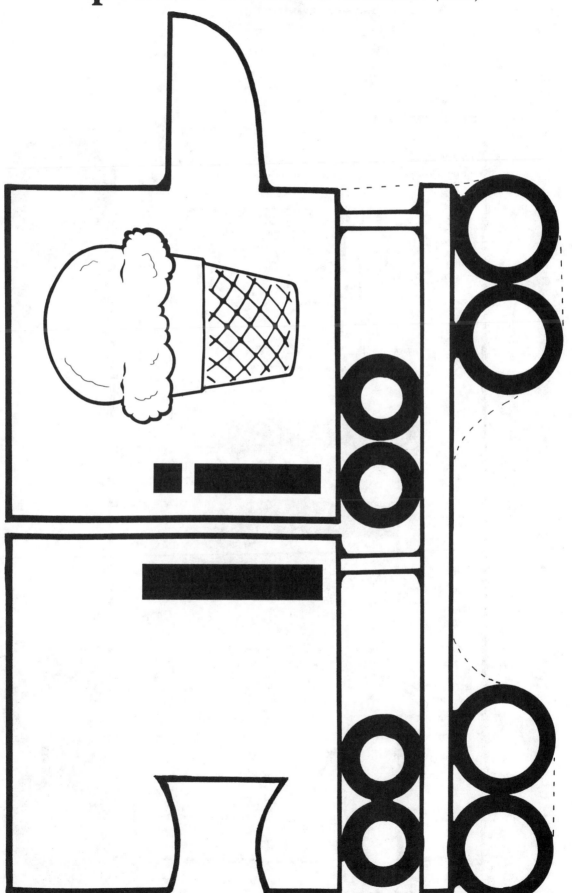

Alphabet Train Puzzle *(cont.)*

Alphabet Train Puzzle (cont.)

Alphabet Train Puzzle (cont.)

Alphabet Train Puzzle (cont.)

Alphabet Train Puzzle (cont.)

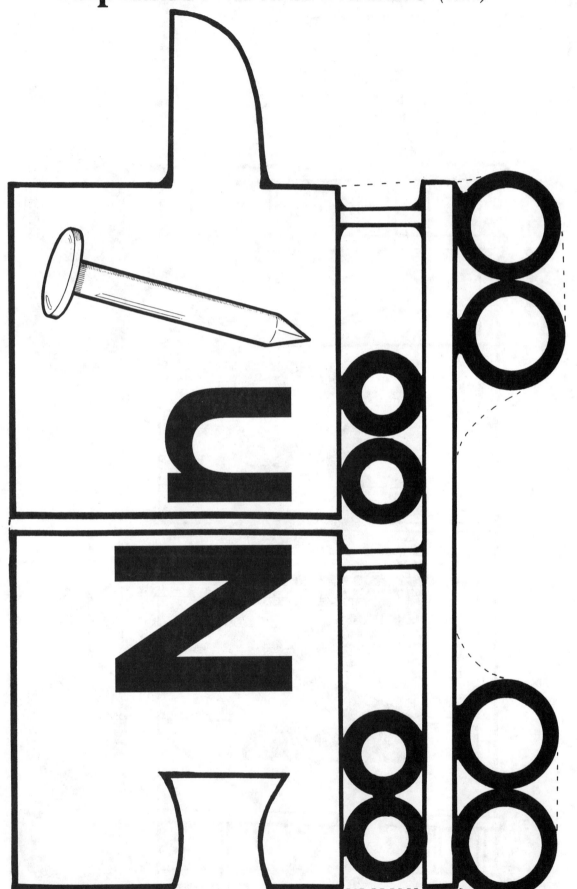

Alphabet Train Puzzle (cont.)

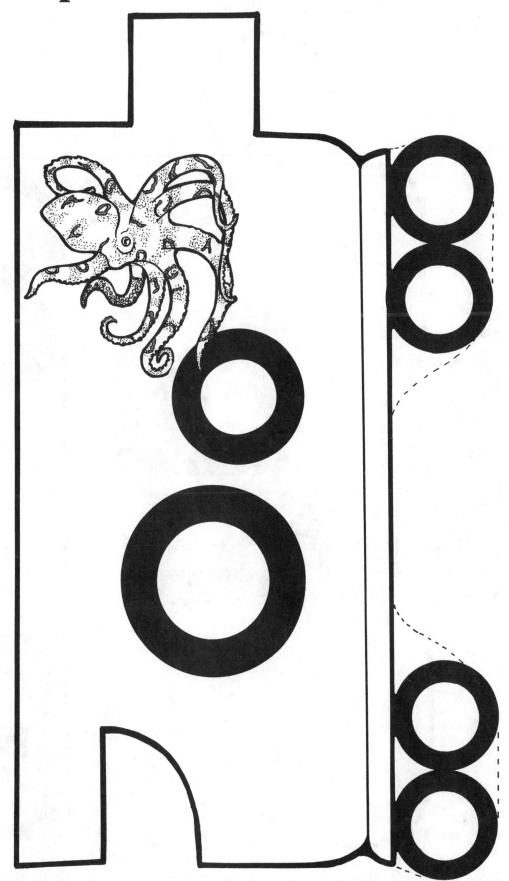

Alphabet Train Puzzles (cont.)

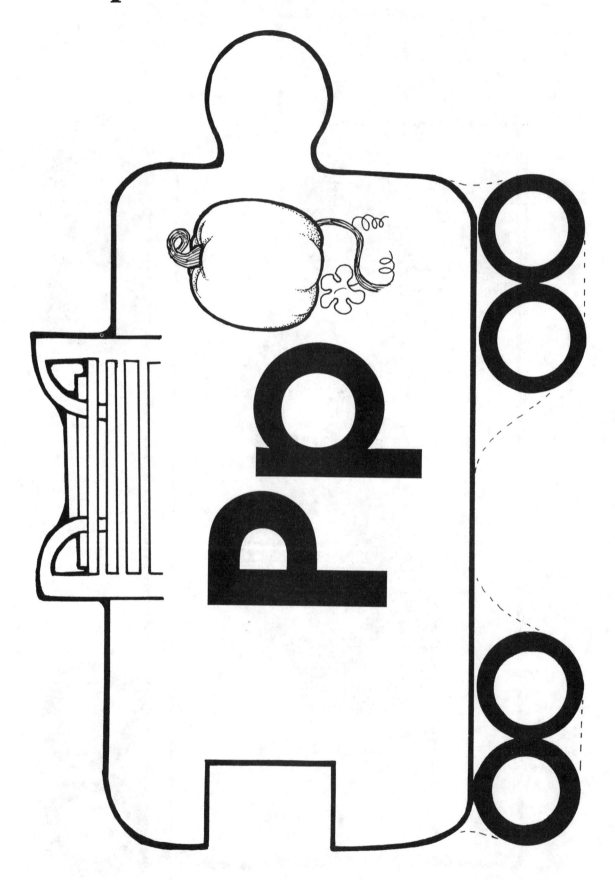

Alphabet Train Puzzle *(cont.)*

Alphabet Train Puzzle *(cont.)*

Alphabet Train Puzzle (cont.)

Alphabet Train Puzzle (cont.)

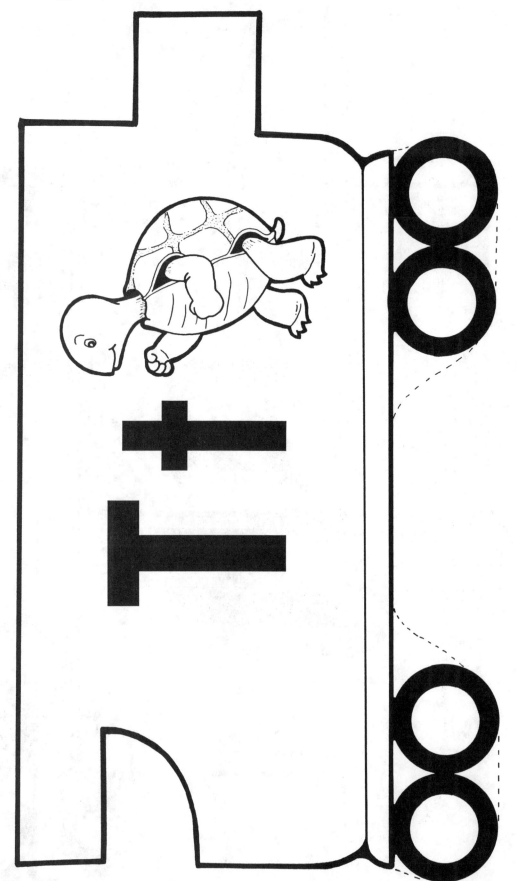

Alphabet Train Puzzle (cont.)

Alphabet Train Puzzle *(cont.)*

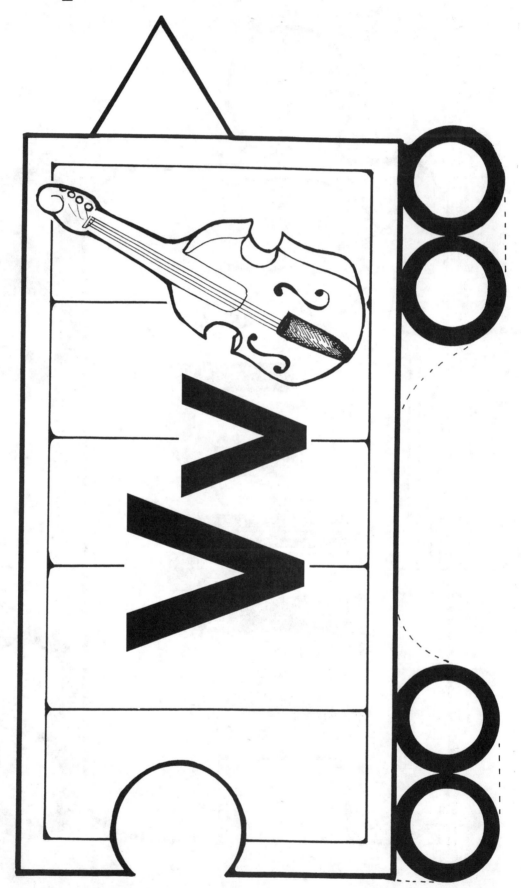

44

Alphabet Train Puzzle (cont.)

Alphabet Train Puzzle *(cont.)*

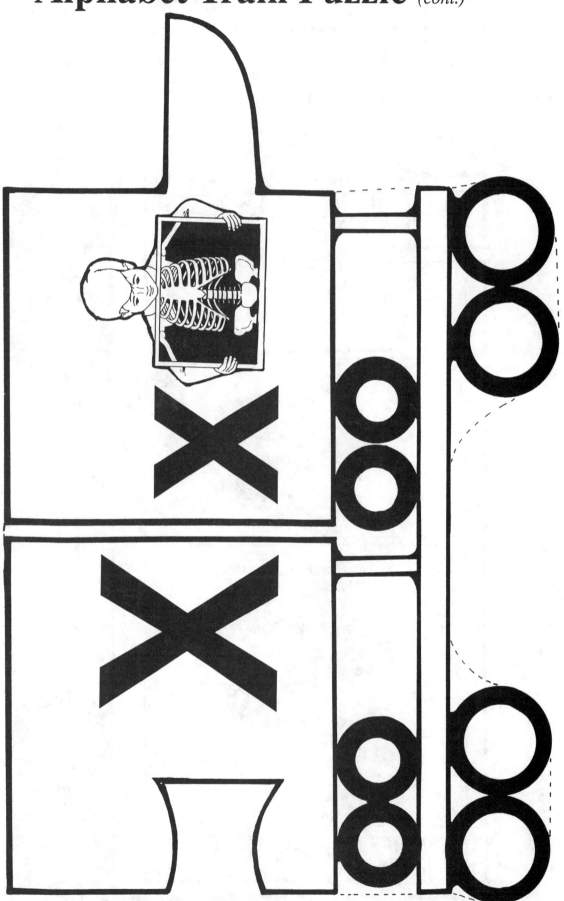

Alphabet Train Puzzle (cont.)

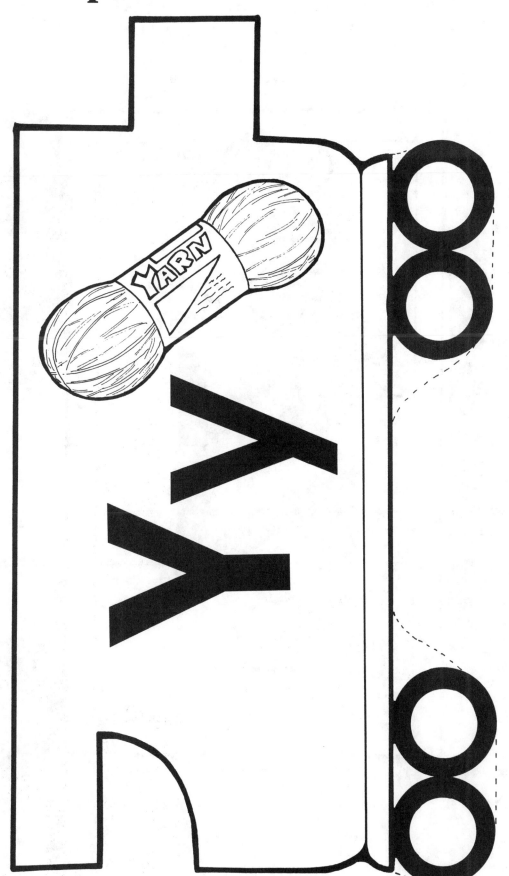

Alphabet Train Puzzle (cont.)

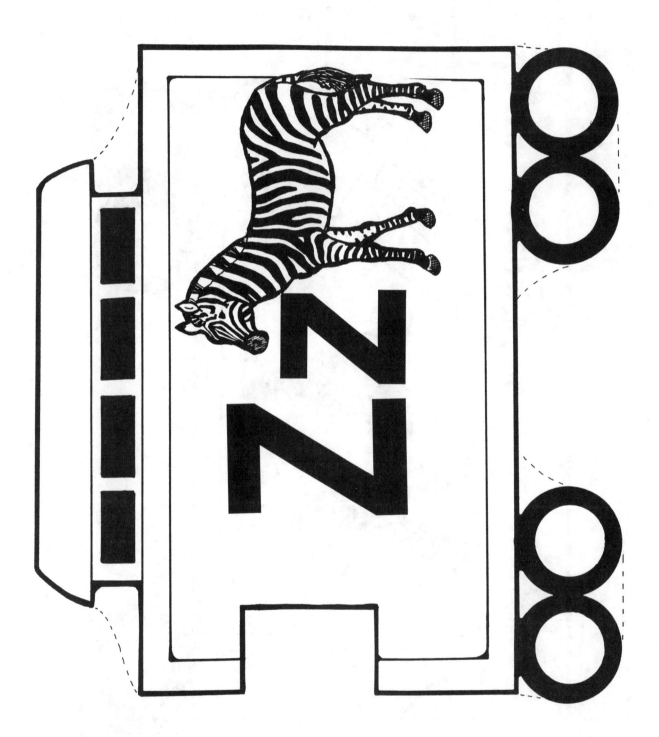

Penny Count Center

Purpose

Through counting a set of pennies, the learner can recognize an amount and assign a number of cents to a set.

Materials

- Paper or real pennies (page 52)
- Ten film containers with lids numbered one to ten
- One pencil
- Recording sheets
- An answer key stored in an envelope

Preparation

Fill ten film containers with sets of pennies appropriate for your class. Number the lids 1-10. Fill in the answer key and place it in the envelope.

Instructions

Children select film container number one, remove the lid and count the pennies in the container. They record the number of pennies in the container on the answer sheet in the appropriate space. After returning the pennies to the container, they continue to count the pennies in the remaining containers.

Clean-Up

Put all pennies in their appropriate container. Make sure the lids are sealed. Remove the answer sheet from the envelope and check your answers.

Helpful Hints

This center can be used again throughout the year by changing the coins to nickels, dimes, quarters, or by using different coins in each container.

Penny Count Center

Answer Key

Reproduce an answer key and place in an envelope. Change it each time you change the number of pennies in a container.

Penny Count Key			
Container	**Penny Count**	**Container**	**Penny Count**
#1		#1	
#2		#2	
#3		#3	
#4		#4	
#5		#5	
#6		#6	
#7		#7	
#8		#8	
#9		#9	
#10		#10	
Container	**Penny Count**	**Container**	**Penny Count**
#1		#1	
#2		#2	
#3		#3	
#4		#4	
#5		#5	
#6		#6	
#7		#7	
#8		#8	
#9		#9	
#10		#10	

Name _____

My Penny Count Recording Sheet

Take a container. Count out the pennies. Record the amount of pennies next to the container number.

Container	Penny Count
#1	
#2	
#3	
#4	
#5	
#6	
#7	
#8	
#9	
#10	

Pennies

Seasons of an Apple Tree

Purpose
Using a set of four picture cards, the learner can match the picture of an apple tree to the season.

Materials
- One set of four apple tree picture cards
- Oaktag
- Storage envelope
- Season chart
- Scissors
- Crayons
- Sets of smaller apple tree cards

Preparation
Reproduce pages 54 and 56 onto oaktag. Color and laminate. Cut off the season at the bottom of each picture and glue to the back of the card. Reproduce page 55, the small apple cards, for each child.

Instructions
Children should place the four large apple tree picture cards onto the season chart. Have them turn the cards over and self-check work to see if they correctly matched the picture to the season. Have each take a sheet of small apple tree cards and color, cut out and label their own set with the name of the season.

Clean-Up
Return the set of apple cards to the storage envelope. Put supplies away.

Helpful Hints
Make additional sets of cards for other types of trees or plants. Children can use the "Seasons of an Apple Tree" cards to make a little book.

"Seasons of an Apple Tree" Cards

The apple blossoms begin to grow.

Spring

The apples grow bigger every day.

Summer

The apples are ready to be picked.

Fall

The tree can rest—no more apples.

Winter

Student Cards

Seasons Chart

Spring

Summer

Fall

Winter

Apples in a Tree

Purpose
The learner will sequence the life of an apple.

Materials
- Apple Tree and Apples
- Scissors
- Glue
- Crayons

Preparation
Reproduce pages 58 and 59.

Instructions
Have children color the tree and pictures. Then cut the apples. They bend them at the flaps and glue the flap onto the correct apple in the tree.

Clean-Up
Make sure there are plenty of trees and flaps for each student.

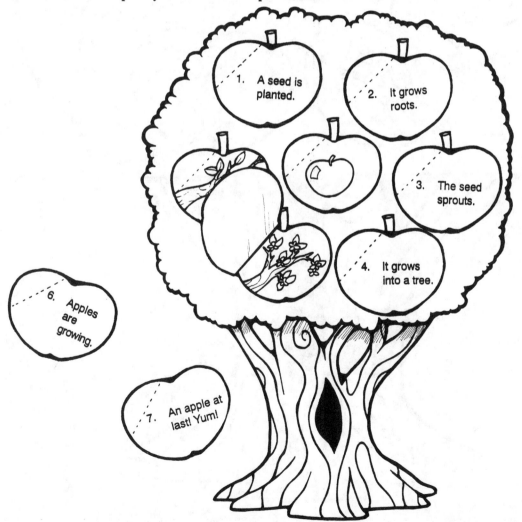

Apples in a Tree

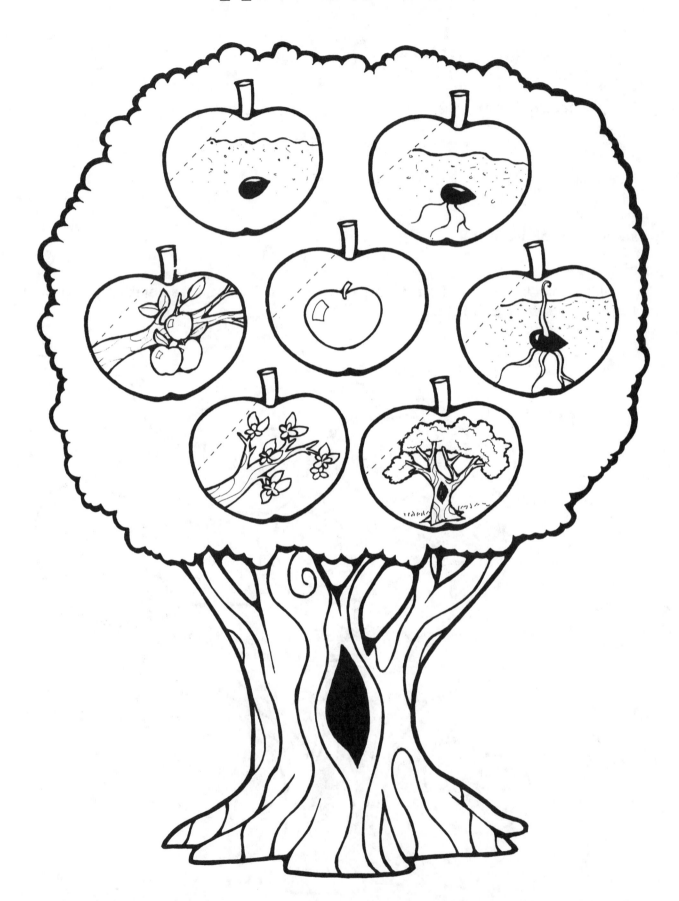

Apples in a Tree *(cont.)*

Apples

1. Color and cut out the apples.

2. Glue the flaps to the matching shapes on the tree.

3. Bend back at the dotted line to watch the apple seed grow.

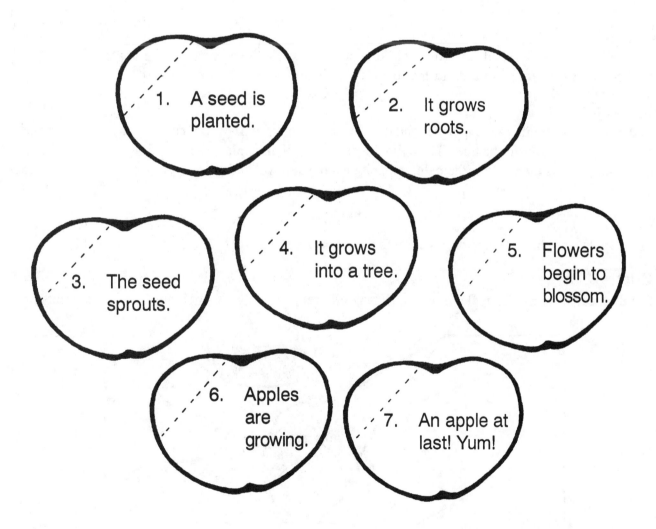

Apple Prints

Purpose

Children can create a picture of an apple tree during spring, summer, fall, and winter, by using an apple to make prints.

Materials

- Apples
- Plastic knife
- Red, yellow, and green paint
- Paper
- Newspaper
- Crayons
- Art smock or paint shirt

Preparation

Cut apples into halves or, if desired, let children use a plastic knife and quarter the apple. (The teacher may choose to cut apples ahead of time so children do not need to use a knife.)

Instructions

Using a piece of white drawing paper and crayons, have children draw and color the trunk and branches of a tree. Add leaves to the tree. The child then selects half an apple and red, yellow, or green paint. He or she presses the apple in the paint, blots it on a paper towel and presses the apple onto the colored tree.

Clean-Up

Place apple print in a place to dry. Close up paint containers. Prepare center for the next child.

Helpful Hints

Children can also use the apple to make prints in different colors or use their apples to make prints on the tree on page 61.

Apple Print Tree

Use pieces of apples to make apple prints on the tree.

Apple Book

Purpose

Children can read and follow directions for coloring an easy-to-read booklet about apples.

Materials

- Apple books
- Crayons

Preparation

Reproduce pages 63-68. Collate them into a little book. You can make different books by arranging the pages in a different order or by using a different number of pages.

Instructions

Students select an apple booklet and read each page. They follow the directions for coloring the pages the appropriate color. They then share the book with a friend or the class.

Clean-Up

Make sure all booklets are put away neatly and that there are booklets ready for the next students who come to the center.

Little Apple Book (cont.)

My Apple Book

Apples

Little Apple Book *(cont.)*

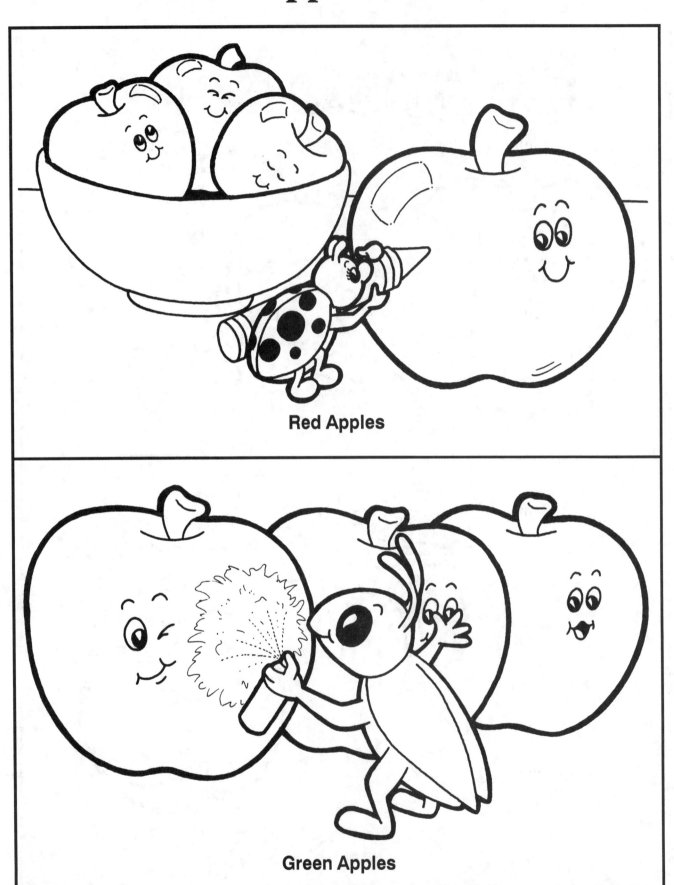

Red Apples

Green Apples

Little Apple Book (cont.)

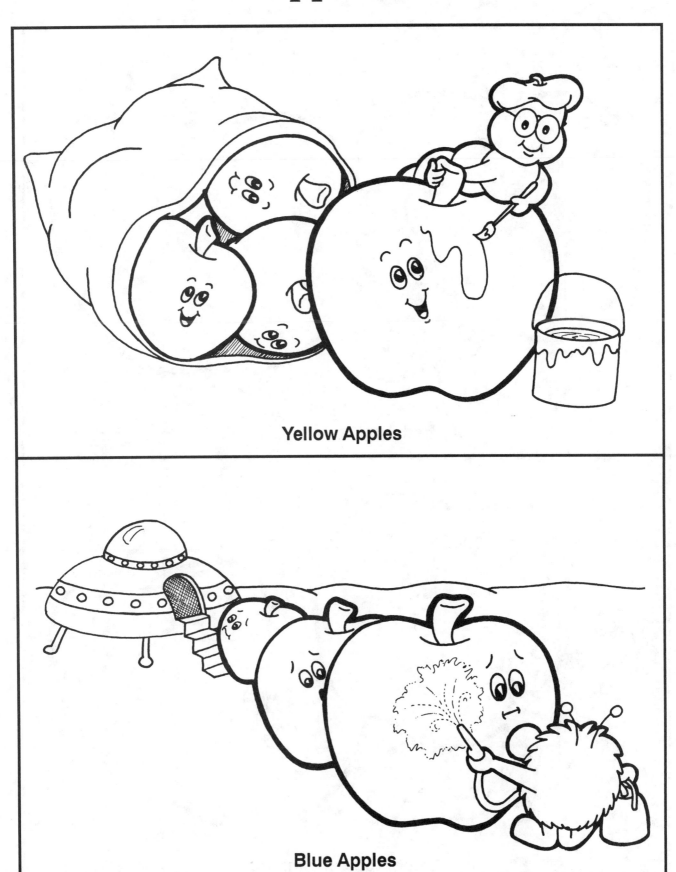

Yellow Apples

Blue Apples

Little Apple Book *(cont.)*

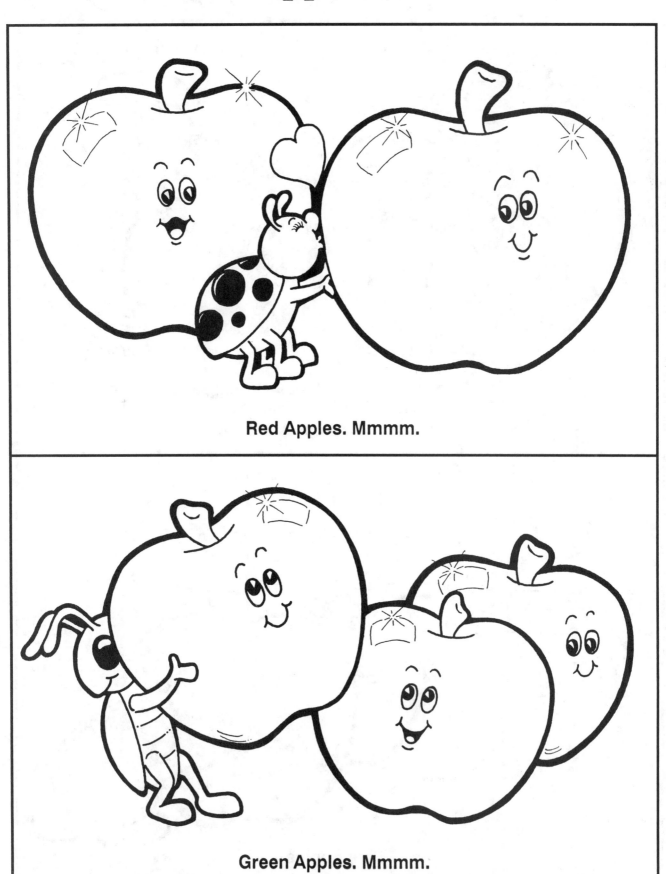

Red Apples. Mmmm.

Green Apples. Mmmm.

Little Apple Book (cont.)

Yellow Apples. Mmmm.

Blue Apples. Yuck!

Little Apple Book *(cont.)*

My favorite apples are _____. Mmmm.

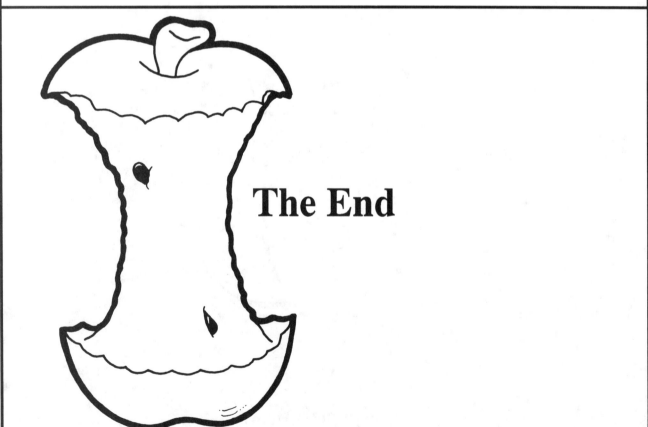

The End

Directions

Purpose

Children begin to learn the four directions: north, south, east, and west.

Materials

- Directions (pages 70)
- Treasure Hunt (page 71)
- Compass pattern (pages 72-74)
- Pencils or crayons

Preparation

Reproduce pages 70-71. Post the *Do You Know Your Directions?* sheet at the center. Set them out with a compass for students to use.

Instructions

Review directions—north, south, east, west—with the students. Show them the compass and how to use it. With a pencil and the chart posted have them complete the treasure hunt.

Clean-Up

Store all materials for the next student to use. Do not allow any magnetic items next to the compass.

Helpful Hints

You may have children make a compass rose of their own or you may wish to make one and leave it at the center for their use.

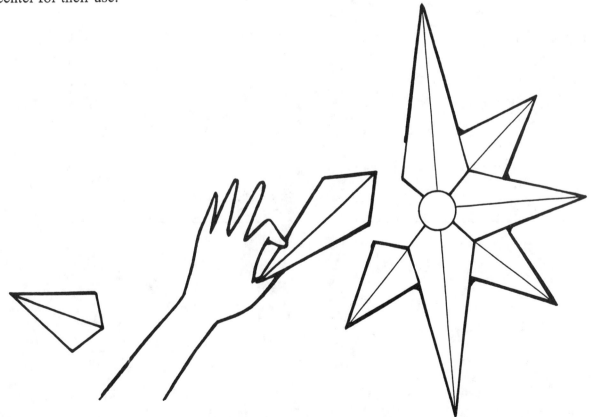

Do You Know Your Directions?

There are four main directions to know as we learn our way around the world in which we live. These directions are north, south, east, and west. These directions make it easier to get around.

Here are what the directions look like on a piece of paper.

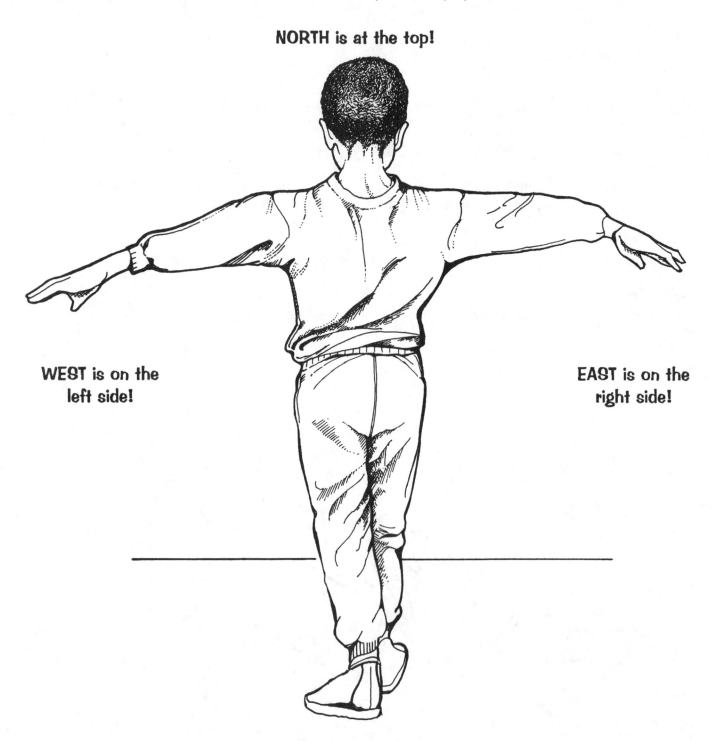

NORTH is at the top!

WEST is on the left side!

EAST is on the right side!

SOUTH is at the bottom!

The Treasure Hunt

A secret treasure has been buried. Color in the footsteps as you follow the directions. The first footprint is the first step.

a.	Take 3 steps east.		d.	Take 3 steps south.
b.	Take 2 steps north.		e.	Take 3 steps west.
c.	Take 2 steps east.			

START

Compass Rose

This is a compass rose. A compass rose is a symbol mapmakers use to show direction.

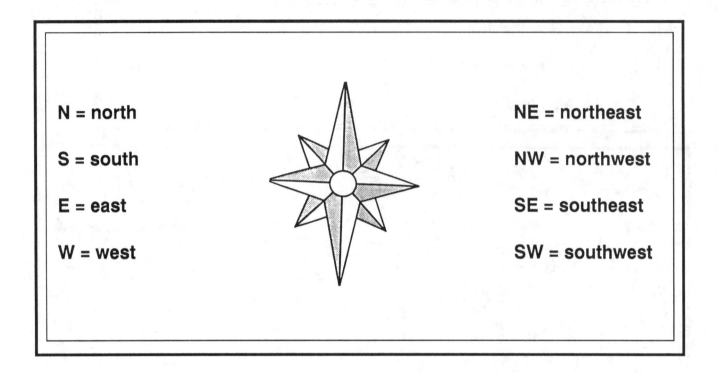

N = north

S = south

E = east

W = west

NE = northeast

NW = northwest

SE = southeast

SW = southwest

1.   Cut out all the pieces for the compass rose.

2.   Arrange them correctly on a large piece of paper.

3.   Attach the pieces in their correct spots with glue or paste.

4.   Label the directional points on the paper.

5.   Color your compass rose.

The north and south points are longer than the other directional points.

Compass Rose *(cont.)*

Compass Rose *(cont.)*

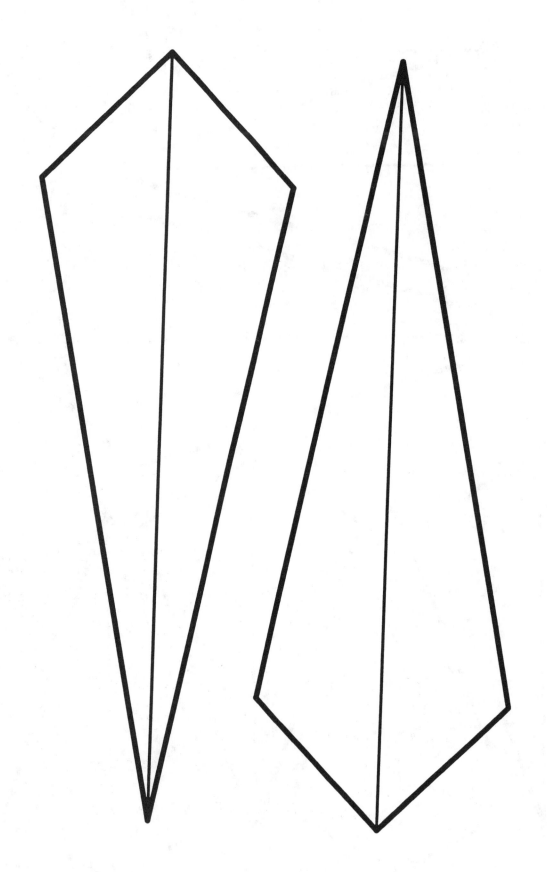

Write a Tall Tale

Purpose

Children will write and illustrate their own tall tale.

Materials

- Story paper (pages 381- 383)
- Pencils
- Books of Tall Tales

Preparation

Read the story of Johnny Appleseed to the children. *Johnny Appleseed* by Steven Kellogg (Morrow, 1988) and *The Story of Johnny Appleseed* by Aliki (Prentice, 1963) are two you may use. As a quick reference, you can reproduce page 76 and leave it for children to refer to, and remind them about Johnny Appleseed and how a real person becomes a character in a tall tale. These may also be left at the center as reference. Other books of tall tales should also be made available to the children.

Instructions

Tell children to think about the story of *Johnny Appleseed*. They can brainstorm their own character and write a tall tale. Each should illustrate his/her own story and be prepared to share it.

Clean-Up

Return all books to their proper place at the center.

Helpful Hints

Use the book cover on page 77. Students may use it individually or you may wish to use it and create a class book of tall tales to leave at the center.

Johnny Appleseed

Johnny Appleseed was born on September 26, 1774. As a boy he learned about apples at a nearby orchard. He walked through Pennsylvania and cleared the land to make way for more orchards. When Johnny grew older, he set out to explore the wilderness in the West. Legend has it Johnny slept in a treetop hammock and played with a bear family. In his later years, Johnny continued to move west and even planted trees in Ohio. During the month of March, in 1845, he became ill and died.

Tall Tale Book Cover

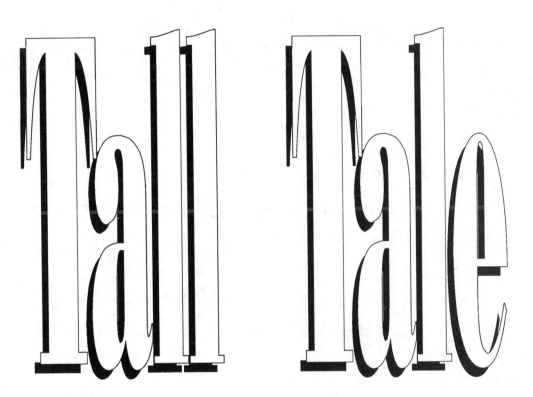

Written by: _____

Play Dough

Purpose

The learners will enhance fine-motor abilities by kneading play dough with their hands and fingers. By using their arms to roll the play dough, the children will also strengthen their gross motor abilities. Playing with play dough relaxes children.

Materials

- Play dough (purchased or homemade)
- Plastic container with lid
- Pizza pan or plastic tray
- Rolling pin

- Plastic cookie cutters (various shapes/sizes)
- Plastic bag for storing cookie cutters
- Backgrounds (pages 79- 81)

Preparation

Prepare homemade play dough by following the recipe below.

Homemade Play Dough Recipe

- 1 cup (250 mL) flour
- 1 cup (250 mL) water
- $^{1}/_{2}$ cup (125 mL) salt

- 1 tablespoon (15 mL) cream of tartar
- 1 tablespoon (15 mL) cooking oil
- a few drops of food coloring

Mix together in a pan and cook on high, stirring constantly. Remove from heat when play dough reaches the correct consistency. Cool.

Instructions

Children can roll the play dough with the rolling pin. They can cut out various shapes using cookie cutters. Children may also use their imaginations to mold and create figures that will fit into the backgrounds provided. These may be glued onto file folders to make them stand up. The objects can be placed in front of them.

Clean-Up

Children must keep the play dough on the pizza pan or tray. All items at this center must be cleaned off when finished. Tightly seal play dough in the container. Place all cookie cutters in a basket or bag. Store all materials at this center on the pizza pan or tray.

Zoo Background

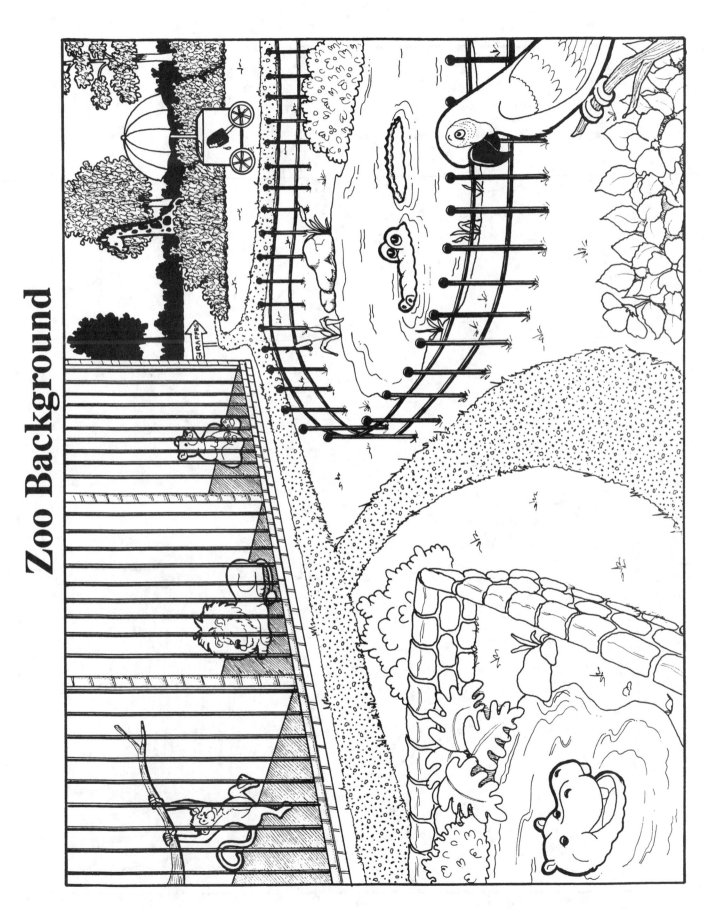

Park Background

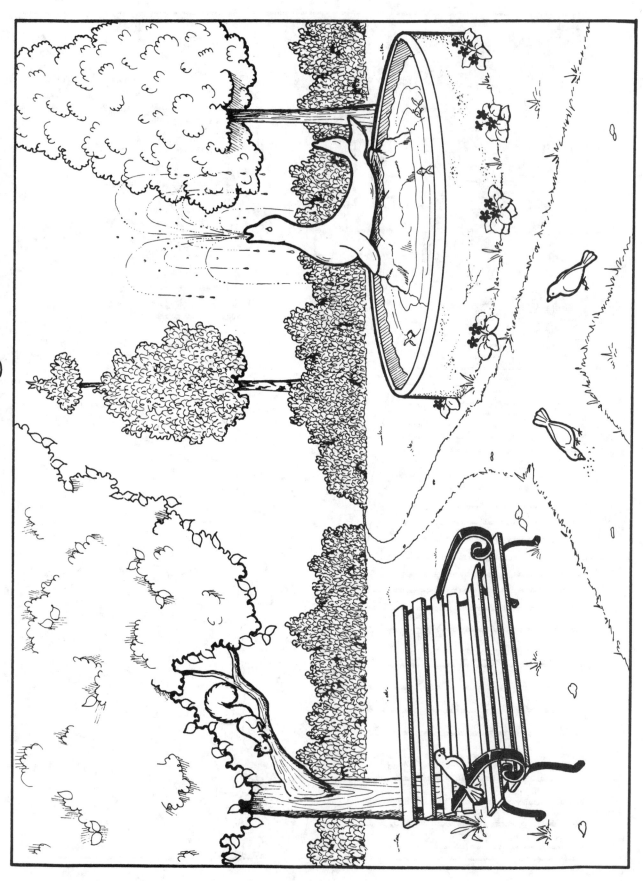

Beach Background

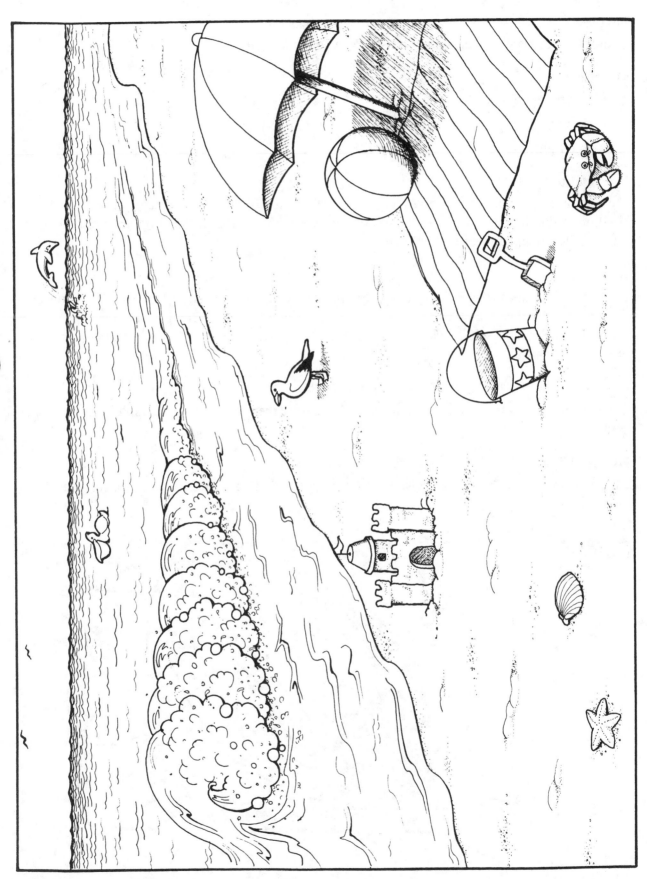

Newspaper Search

Purpose

Children will locate a given sight word in a newspaper clipping.

Materials

- Newspaper clippings
- Envelopes
- Highlighter

Preparation

Cut several articles out of the newspaper. Sort them into different envelopes. Choose a word you want children to find in the article. Write it on the envelope. At the top of the clipping, write the number of times the word will appear in the article.

Instructions

Children select an envelope. They study the word on the envelope and say the word to themselves. They take a clipping from the envelope and locate the word in the clipping, going over the word with a highlighter. Students self-check by seeing if the amount of words found match the number written at the top of the article.

Clean-Up

Students can take articles back to their seats. Make sure there are plenty of clippings in envelopes for students to choose.

Helpful Hints

Children may take clippings to their seats. Challenge them to use a sight word in a sentence.

Rhyming Words

Purpose
By playing this game, children review rhyming words and match rhyming pictures.

Materials
- Game pieces (pages 84 - 87)
- Manila envelope

Preparation
Reproduce and cut the cards. Color and laminate. Store the cards in the manila envelope.

Instructions
Spread out the game pieces and match the pictures that rhyme. The teacher will check students work.

Clean-Up
Place all rhyming game pieces in the envelope.

Helpful Hints
Students can self-check the game if matching symbols or colored dots are placed on the back of matching cards.

As an extension have students create their own rhyming word cards.

Rhyming Word Game Pieces

Rhyming Word Game Pieces *(cont.)*

Rhyming Word Game Pieces (cont.)

Rhyming Word Game Pieces *(cont.)*

Button Sort

Purpose
The child will discriminate among different colors of buttons and sort them into groups, recognizing each color word as a name of a group.

Materials
- Can with a lid
- Ten small paper cups

Preparation
Label the ten paper cups with the following color words: red, blue, green, yellow, orange, black, brown, gray, pink, white. Write the number of each color of buttons that should be placed in the cup on the bottom. Put the correct number of each color buttons for each cup in the can.

Instructions
Set out the ten cups labelled with color words on the table. Open the can containing the buttons. Have children take out several buttons and sort them, by color, into the cups. They should continue to work until all the buttons are sorted. When all the buttons are in the cups, have the children look at the bottom of each cup for a number. For self-checking this number will indicate how many buttons should be in that cup. For example, the cup labelled red may have the number 8 on the bottom. This means there should be 8 red buttons in the cup.

Clean-Up
Empty all cups into the button storage can. Close up the button can and stack all the cups.

Helpful Hints
Send a note to parents at the beginning of the school year asking them to send in buttons of the specified colors for help when setting up this center. See page 360 for a letter to send home.

The button sort tree on page 89 can be used as an extension of this center. Students may sort the buttons onto the tree branches based on the colors, the number of holes, or the size of the buttons.

Button Tree

Leaf Sort and Classify

Purpose

Given a set of cards with pictures of various leaves on them the child can sort leaves by color, shapes, and then according to smooth or toothed edges.

Materials:

- A set of leaf cards (pages 91-94)
- An envelope for storage
- Crayons

Preparation

Reproduce the leaf cards onto index paper. Color those on page 91 different colors.   Color all other leaves the same. Laminate and cut out. Place a set of all the cards into an envelope.

Instructions

Have children remove all of the leaf cards from the storage envelopes. They begin sorting cards by color, then they sort the leaves by shape, and finally by smooth or toothed edges.

Clean-Up

Return all leaf cards to the storage envelope.

Helpful Hints

This activity can be done with real leaves, if enough different types are available.

Leaves - Different Colors

Leaves - Different Shapes

Leaves - Smooth Edge

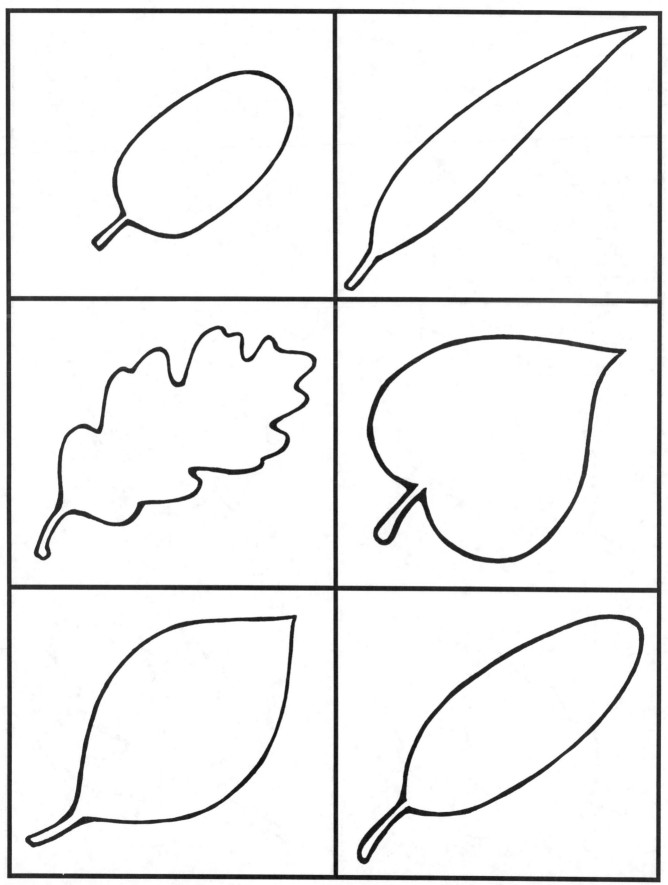

Leaves - Tooth Edge

Leaf Rubbings

Purpose

By making leaf rubbings, children can compare different types of leaves.

Materials

- Leaves from various trees
- Newsprint
- Masking tape
- Peeled crayons or colored chalk (brown, orange, red, yellow, and green)

Preparation

Collect fallen leaves. Find as many different types as possible. Tape one down for students to use in order to create a rubbing.

Instructions

Tape a leaf to the table. Have students put a piece of newsprint over it. Let them use the side of a peeled crayon or piece of chalk and rub it gently over the leaf several times until a leaf appears. Let children compare the rubbings they did with others to compare whether they used the same type of leaf or a different one.

Clean-Up

Make sure leaves are removed from the table and different ones are taped down.

Helpful Hints

These leaf rubbings will create a nice bulletin board.

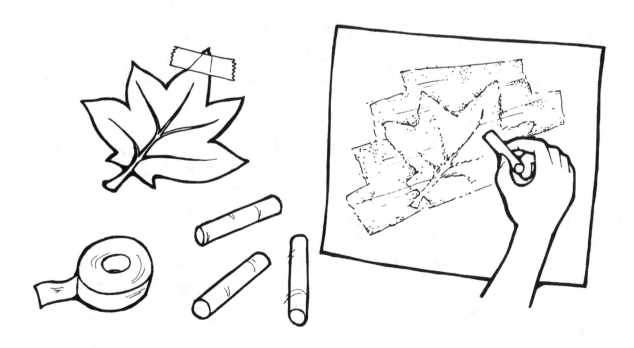

Line Drawing

Purpose
Given a line on a piece of white drawing paper, learners will use their imaginations to create a picture.

Materials
- White drawing paper 8 ½" x 11" (22 cm x 28 cm) with a black line on it
- Black marker or crayon
- Crayons or markers

Preparation
Take a black marker and make straight or curved lines on the white paper. Students will then select a sheet to make into a picture.

Instructions
Students take one piece of drawing paper. Have them study the black line on the page. Tell them to turn the paper horizontally or vertically, depending on what they plan to create out of the line. Encourage them to use their imaginations to make the line into a picture. Have teacher color their pictures and be ready to tell classmates about their line drawing.

Clean-Up
Make sure children put their names on the back of the line drawing picture and return the crayons or markers to their containers.

Create a Monster Mask

Purpose
Children will use their imaginations to create a monster mask.

Materials
- Patterns (pages 98-101)
- Paper plates sheets
- Scissors
- Crayons and markers
- *Where The Wild Things Are* or other monster story

Preparation
Reproduce the patterns. Prepare paper plates by putting in eye holes and string to wrap them around the head. Read *Where The Wild Things Are* by Maurice Sendak or any other appropriate story about monsters to the class. Leave the book at the center for the children to refer to.

Instructions
Use the sheets provided. Children select eyes, nose, ears, and mouth. They color the parts and cut them out. They paste them onto a paper plate to create their own monster mask.

Clean-Up
Clean up the area. Throw away scraps and put all supplies away.

Helpful Hints
Students may choose to make their own monster face parts. They may use the patterns as samples.

Monster Noses

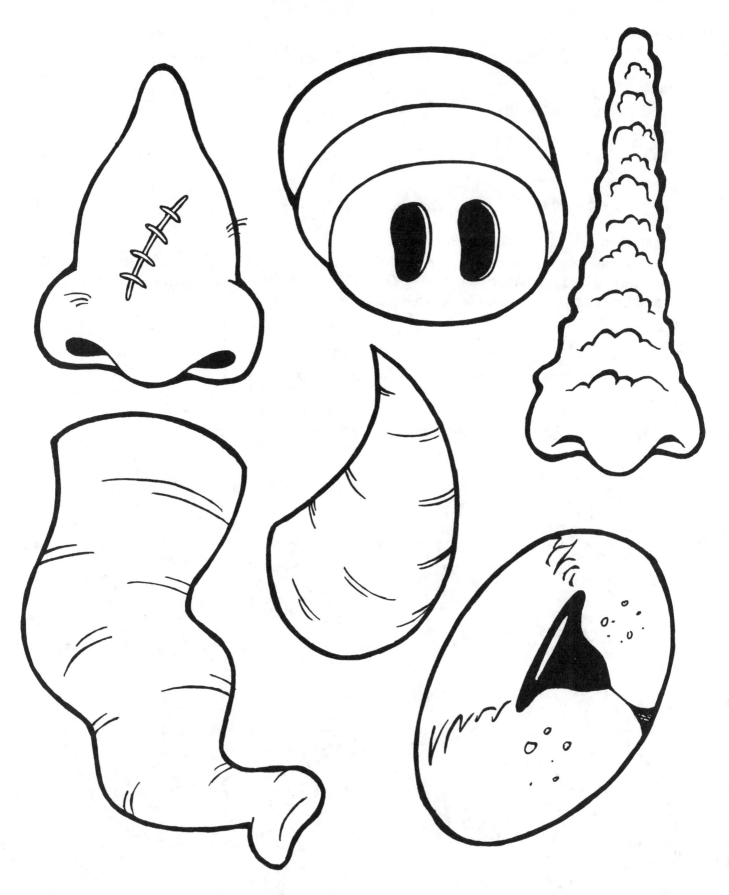

98

Monster Eyes

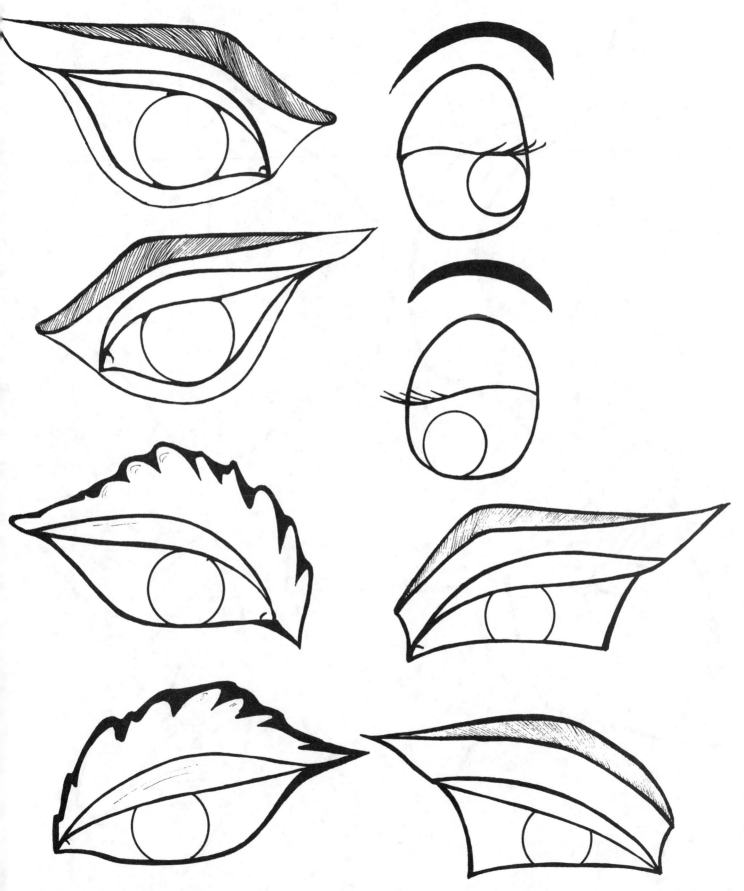

Monster Ears

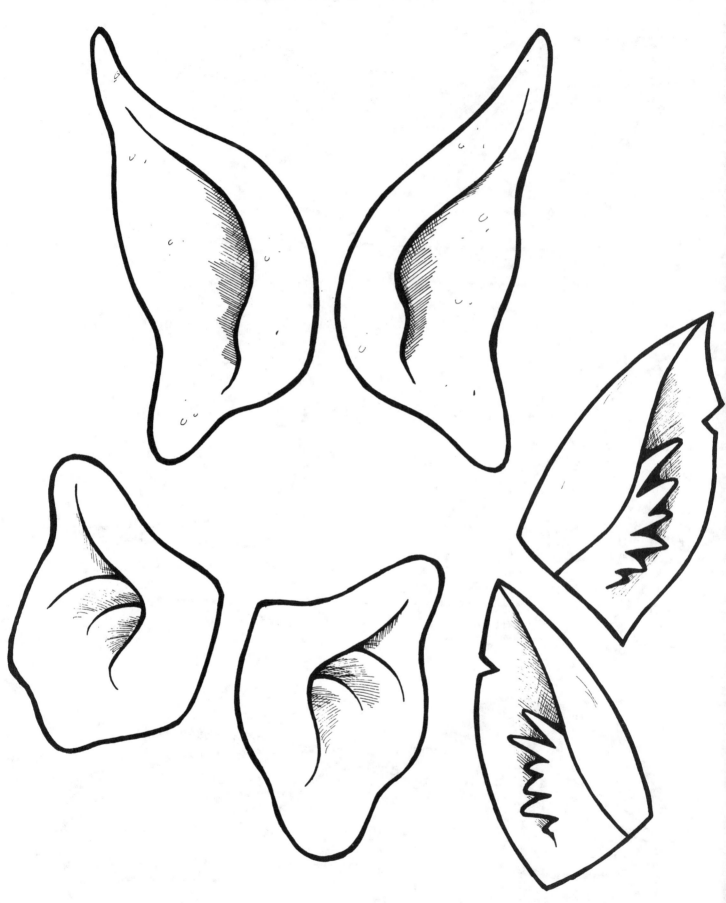

Monster Mouths

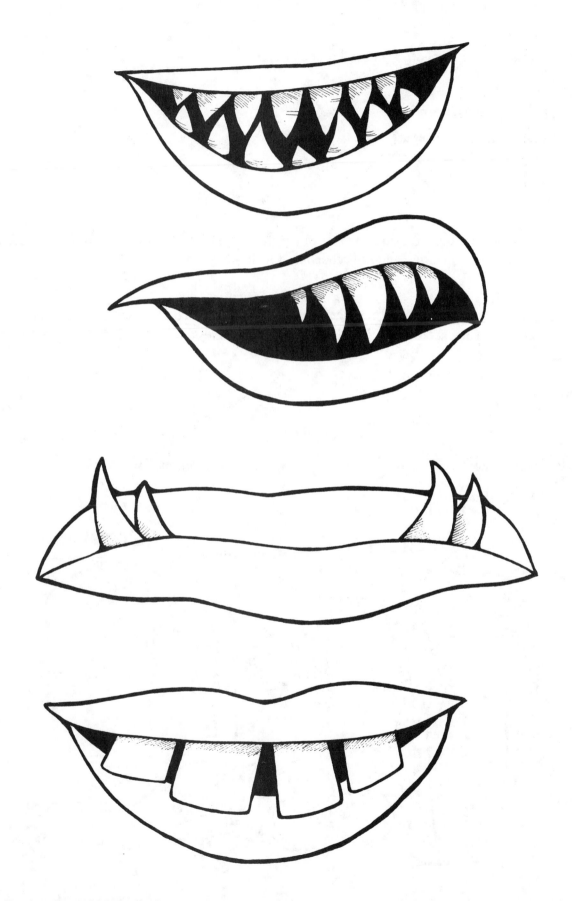

Fire Safety

Purpose

Children will practice the stop, drop, and roll procedure.

Materials

- Rug or a sleeping bag
- Chart illustrating the procedure (pages 103-104)
- Small chart (page 105)
- Crayons

Preparation

Put together the large chart. Color and hang it at the center. Reproduce the small chart, one for each child. Demonstrate the stop, drop, and roll procedure for the children.

Instructions

Children practice the stop, drop, and roll procedure illustrated by the chart. They use the sleeping bag as their practice area. They should practice the procedure five times and then color a chart to take back to their seats.

Clean-Up

Leave the sleeping bag unrolled.

Helpful Hints

Post the large chart showing the correct procedures and steps. Children may make the fire fighter's hat on page 106.

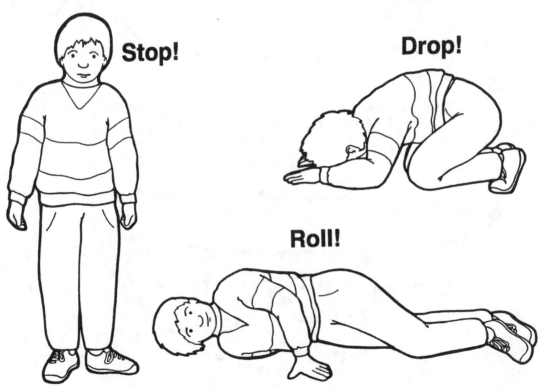

Drop!

Roll!

Stop!

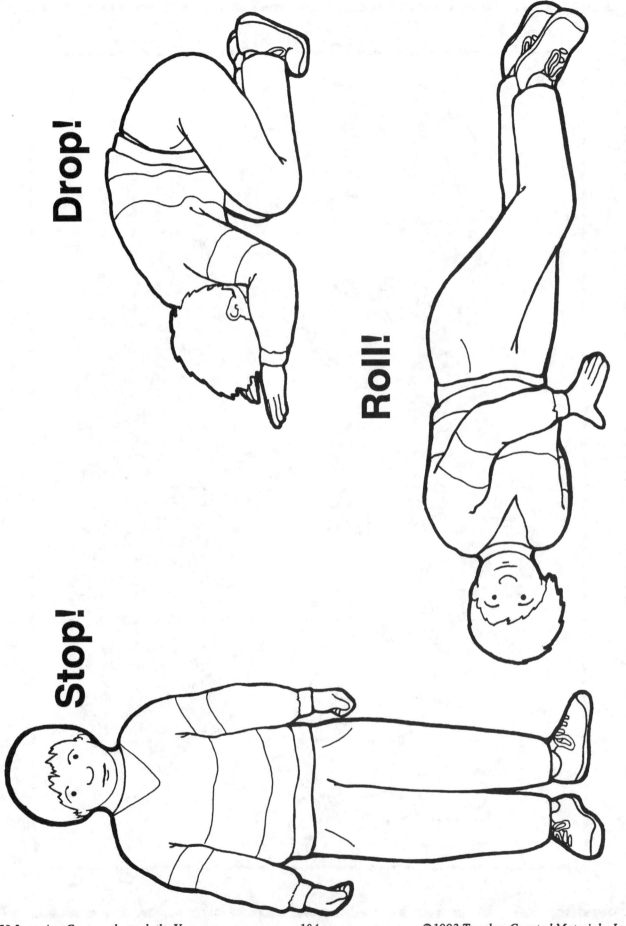

Fire Safety

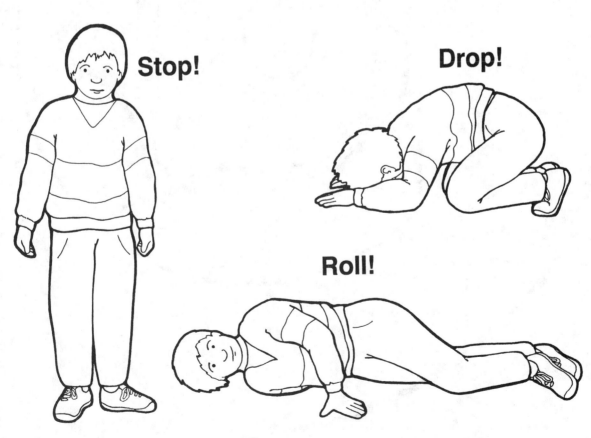

Stop!

Drop!

Roll!

Firefighters Hat Pattern

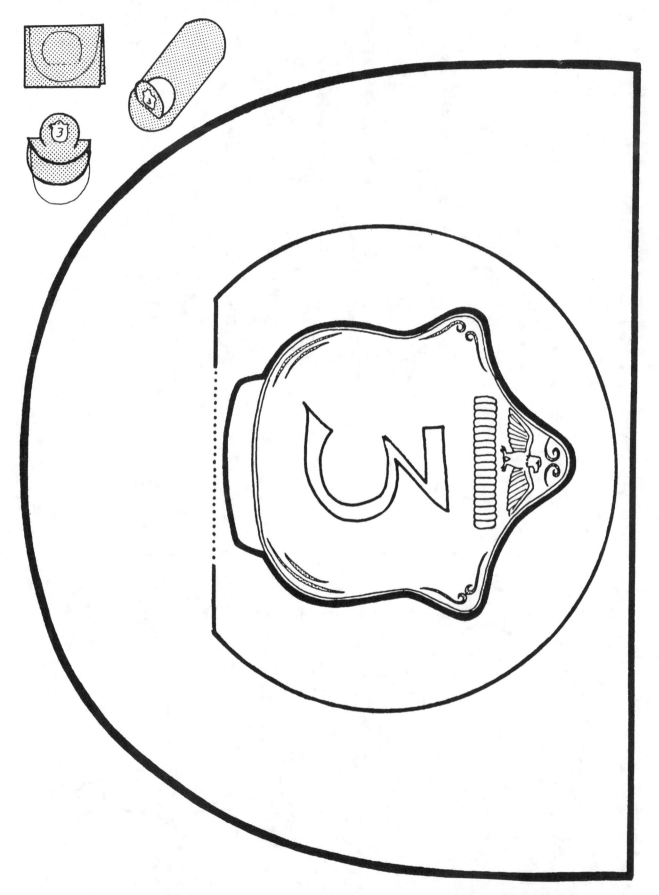

Monster Story Starters

Purpose

Given a set of story starters children can create a story about monsters.

Materials

- Writing utensils
- Story paper (pages 381-383)
- Story starters (page 108)
- Container

Preparation

Reproduce story starters. You may wish to laminate them before cutting them out and placing them at the center.

Instructions

Students select a story starter about a monster. Using story paper, they begin the story. They brainstorm an ending and illustrate the story with a picture of the monster.

Clean-Up

Return the story starters to the container.

Helpful Hints

Use the blank monster shape on page 108 to create your own story starters.

Monster Story Starters

My monster lives in . . .

My monster looks like . . .

My monster helps me . . .

My monster is not scary
because . . .

My monster is my good
friend because . . .

Dial-It!

Purpose
As part of the fire safety unit, children will practice dialing "911." They will also dial other numbers on the telephone. Children will practice what they would say on the phone in an emergency situation.

Materials
- Old rotary telephone
- Push-key or touch-tone telephone
- Telephone book
- Classroom telephone book

Preparation
Set up the center with the phones. Display the sign that reminds children that 911 is for emergencies only.

Instructions
Have children practice pushing the keys or dialing 911. Then practice telling the appropriate information as if it is an emergency. State name, address, and the situation. After students practice dialing 911, they locate numbers in the telephone book and practice dialing them also.

Clean-Up
Make sure phones are back in place with the receivers hung up.

Helpful Hints
Students should discuss this procedure with their parents, who should reinforce that 911 is only for emergency situations. Children may also make the telephone (pages 111-112) to practice with. They attach the receiver to the base of the phone with a ribbon or string.

911 Sign

In an emergency

Dial 911

Telephone Pattern

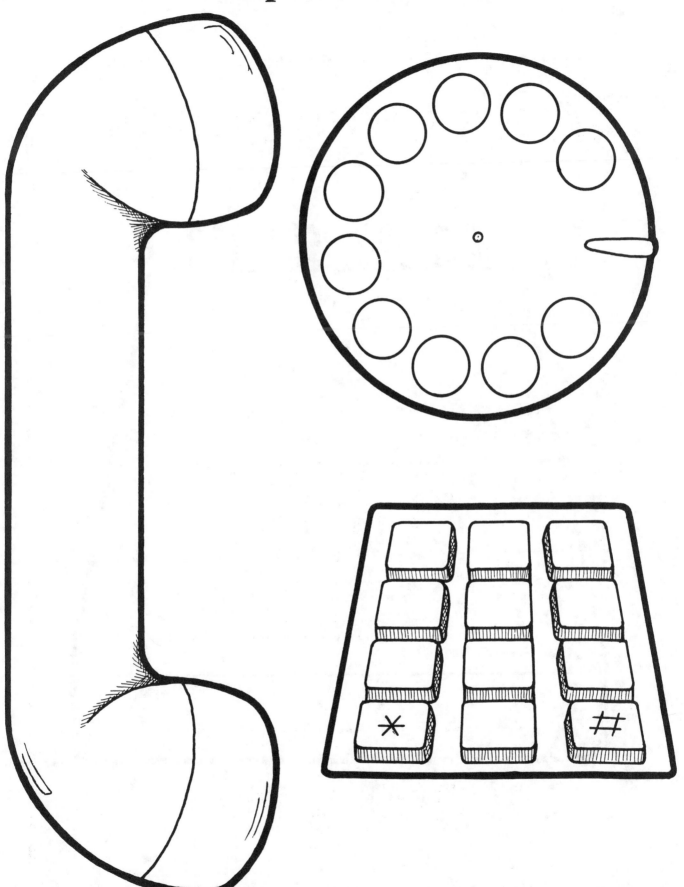

Telephone Pattern *(cont.)*

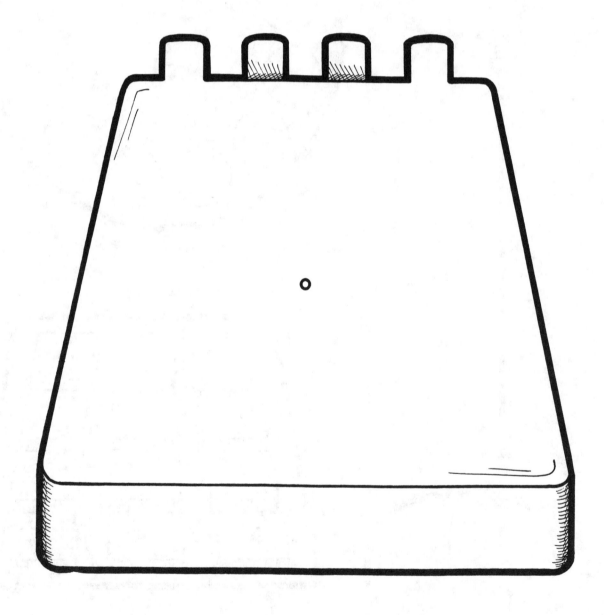

Personal Phone Book

Emergency Numbers

In an emergency dial _____

Fire _____

Police _____

Doctor _____

Dentist _____

Home _____

Mom's Work _____

Dad's Work _____

Neighbor _____

Other Important Numbers

Name	Phone Number
_____	_____
_____	_____
_____	_____
_____	_____

Beginning Sounds Cut and Paste

Purpose
Children find pictures in a magazine that begin with a chosen letter sounds.

Materials
- Drawing paper
- Magazines
- Paste
- Scissors
- Pencil
- Basket for supplies

Preparation
Fold each piece of the drawing paper of the worksheet provided into fourths. With a black marker, write a lower case letter in each section.

Instructions
Give children one piece of prepared paper. Have them put their names on the back. Tell them to look at the letters printed in each square. Search through the magazines provided and find pictures that begin with each letter sound. Cut them out and paste them in the appropriate square.

Clean-Up
Close up the glue or paste. Put magazines in a neat stack. Return all supplies to the basket. Check pictures to see if they begin with the letters.

Helpful Hints
Ask children to bring in old magazines from home for this center. Send home the supply request letter on page 360 or page 361.

Beginning Sounds
Cut and Paste Worksheet

Name _____

Words that start with

Words that start with

Words that start with

Words that start with

Beginning Sound Poke Holes

Purpose
The learner will identify the beginning sound of a picture by saying the name of the picture and poking a finger or a pencil through the hole below the coordinating letter.

Materials
- Cards (pages 117- 118)
- Scissors
- Craft knife
- Crayons or markers
- Storage container

Preparation
Reproduce the cards onto index paper. Circle the hole of the correct answer on the back of the card. Color them. Laminate for durability. Cut out the holes using a craft knife.

Instructions
Have children complete one poke hole at a time. They should say the name of the picture quietly. They will need to poke a finger or a pencil in the hole with the letter that represents the beginning sound. The child will then look at the back of the card to check for the correct answer above the hole with his or her finger.

Clean-Up
After completing and checking each card, return them to their storage container.

Helpful Hints
Use the blank poke hole card on page 119 to create poke hole cards for long and short vowels, final letter sounds, and blends.

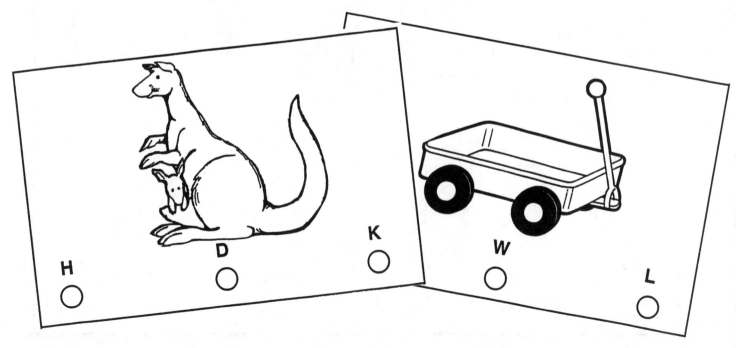

Poke Holes

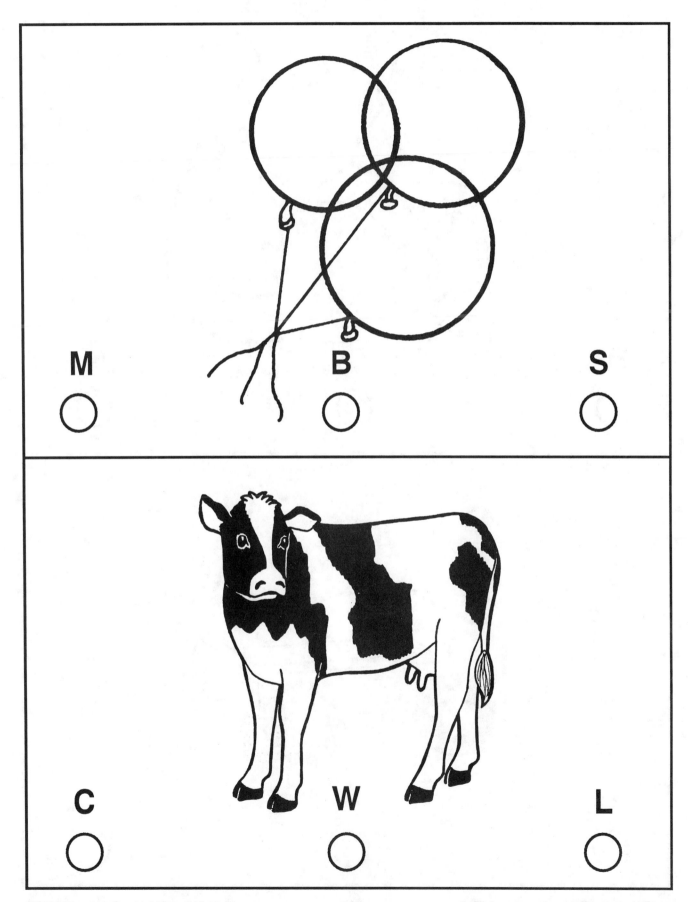

M   **B**   **S**

C   **W**   **L**

Poke Holes (cont.)

H   D   K

G   W   L

Poke Holes *(cont.)*

Roll a Dice Strips

Purpose

Using graph paper cut into prepared strips and a die, the learner will write an addition fact.

Materials:

- Inch or centimeter graph paper cut into strips of 6, 7, 8, and 9 squares or patterns (page 121)
- 1 die (page 122)
- Crayons
- Pencils

Preparation

Cut inch or centimeter graph paper into strips of 6, 7, 8, or 9 squares or use the patterns. Store each set of strips in a separate envelope. Use prepared die or make one using the pattern.

Instructions

Select a 6 strip from an envelope. Roll the die. Color the same number of squares on the strip as was rolled on the die. Then flip the strip over and write an addition number sentence for the 6 strip. For example: A 4 is rolled. Color 4 squares, then write 4 + 2 = 6. Proceed to a 7 strip.

Clean-Up

Put all supplies away and have children take completed fact strips to their seats.

Helpful Hints

Make your own die or dice and you can change the number combinations to equal any fact. You can mark the die with numbers or dots.

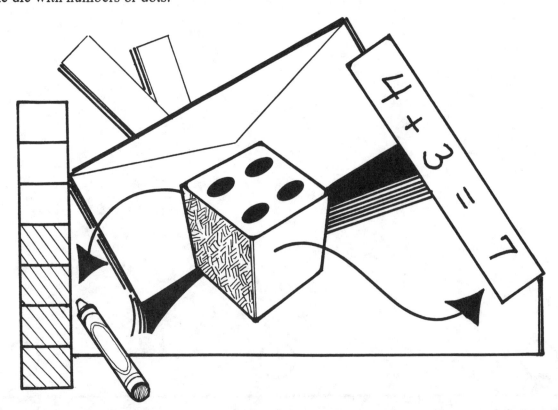

Roll Dice Strips

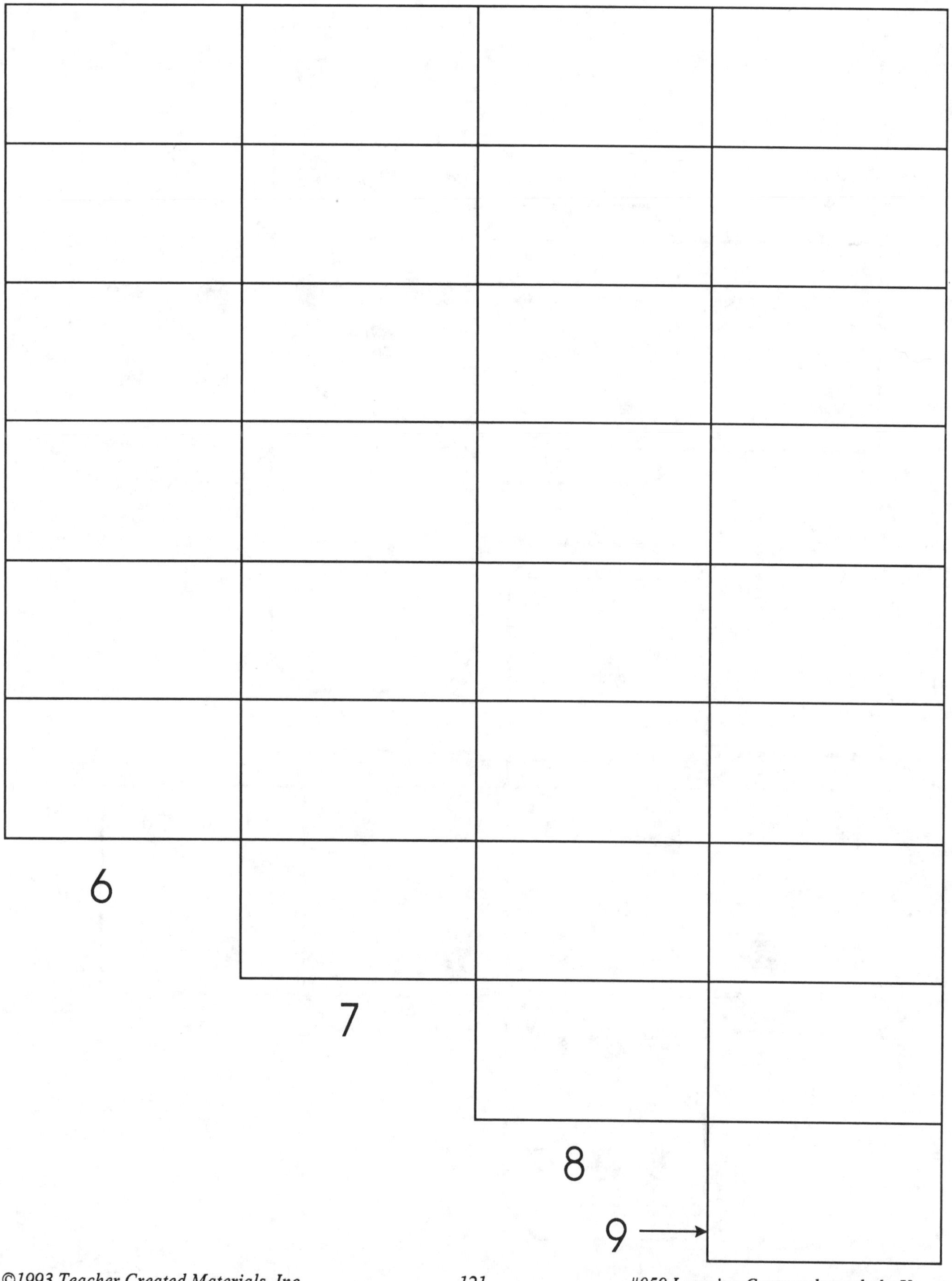

6

7

8

9 →

Dice Pattern

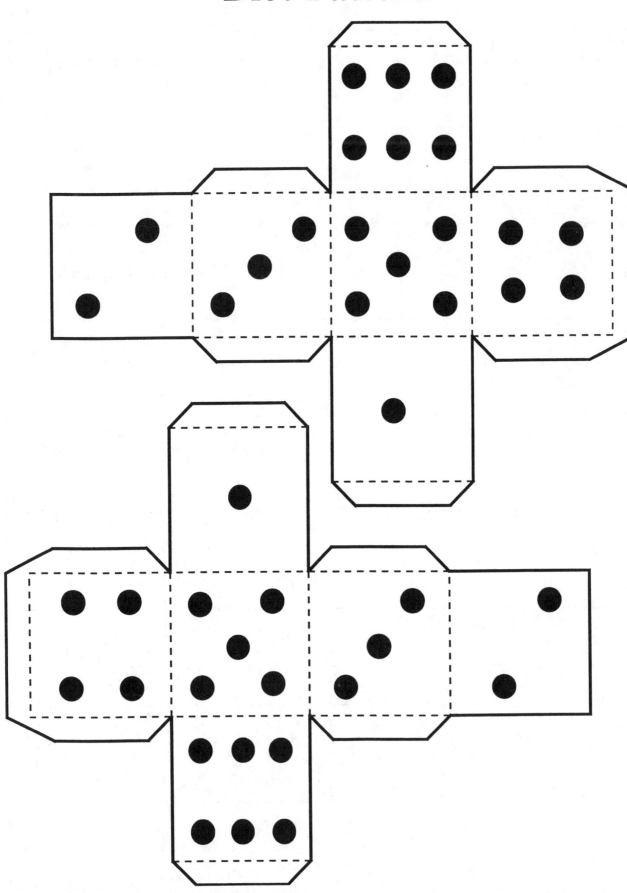

Food Pyramid Cut and Paste

Purpose

Children will look through a magazine or use pictures provided and select pictures of food which they will categorize into the food groups by pasting them onto a prepared food pyramid chart.

Materials

- Magazines or pictures of food (pages 126-127)
- Scissors
- Glue or paste
- Copy of the food guide pyramid (pages 124-125)
- Container for supplies

Preparation

Reproduce the food guide pyramid. Attach the two parts together. Place it, and all other necessary materials in the learning center.

Instructions

Let children search through a magazine for pictures of food, or provide pictures. Have them cut out several and decide where each belongs on the food pyramid. They then paste pictures onto the appropriate areas.

Clean-Up

Make sure all magazines are put in a neat stack and all supplies returned to the container provided. Children may place names on the back of their papers and put completed food pyramids on the chalk tray.

Helpful Hints

As students cut out pictures, have them put their pictures in an envelope so they don't get lost or wind up on the floor.

Pyramids can be checked by classmates and then placed on a classroom bulletin board. Children may also use the place setting on page 128 and put food on the plate that would represent good nutrition. Send home one of the parent request letters on page 360 or 361 requesting magazines.

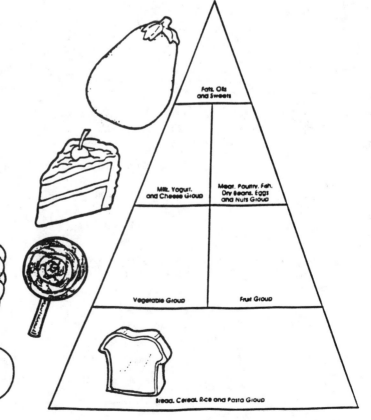

Food Pyramid

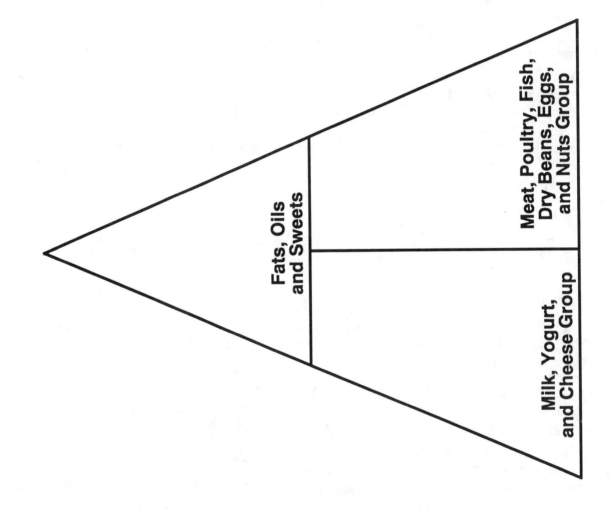

Food Pyramid *(cont.)*

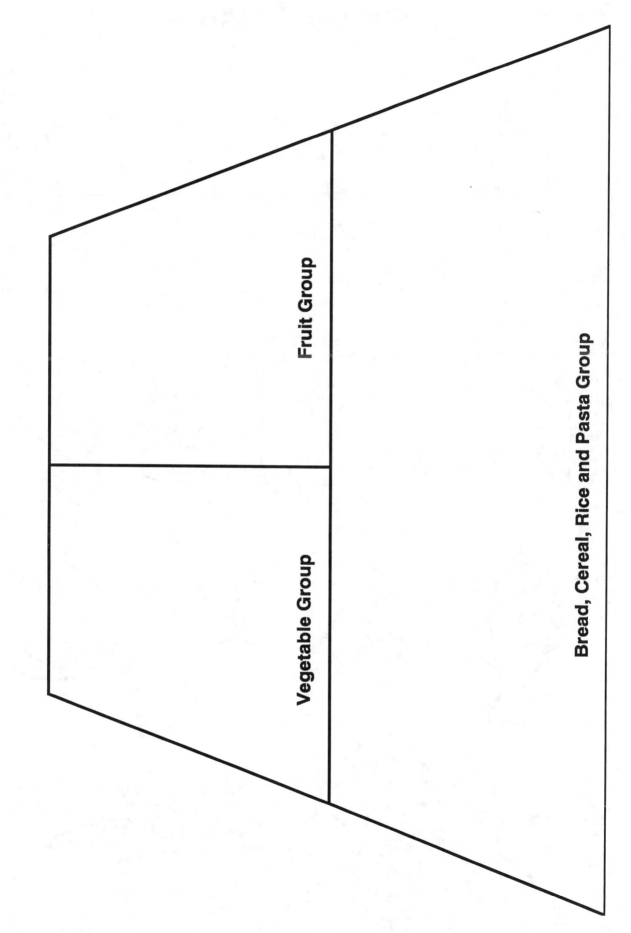

Fruit Group

Vegetable Group

Bread, Cereal, Rice and Pasta Group

Food for Pyramid

Food for Pyramid (cont.)

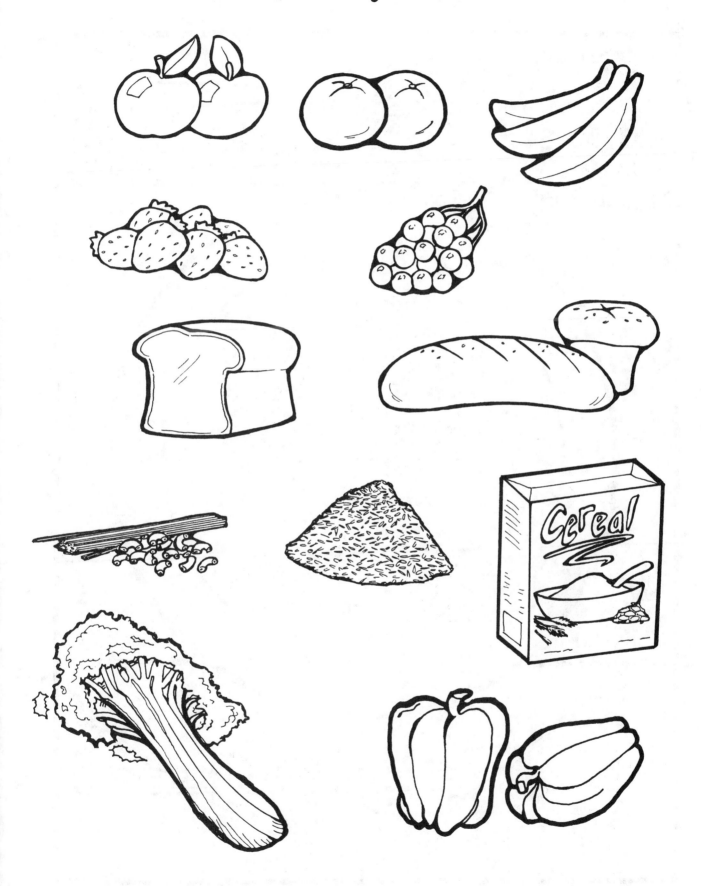

Place Setting

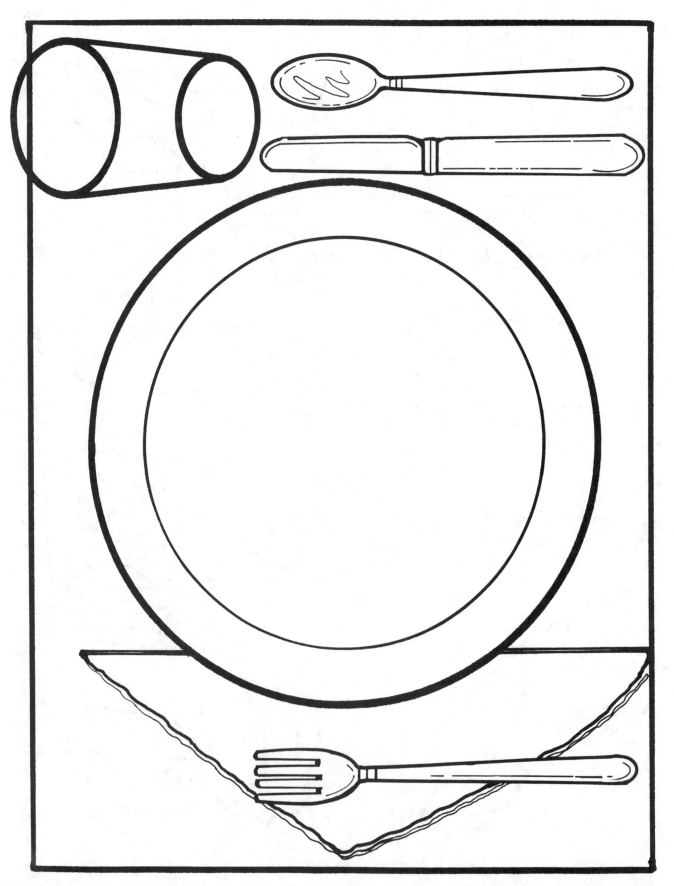

Hats and Headbands

Purpose

Children will become familiar with the hats and headwear associated with Pilgrims and Native Americans, used in conjunction with learning about Thanksgiving.

Materials

- Patterns (pages 130-132)
- Index or Construction Paper (gray, brown, white)
- Crayons
- Stapler

- Tape or glue
- Yarn
- Scissors
- Paper clips

Preparation

Reproduce patterns on pages 130-132 onto appropriately colored index paper or construction paper. Cut out headbands that will fit children's heads. These can be made 2" (5 cm) wide.

Instructions

Pilgrim boy hat: Let children color and cut out the hat, pasting or taping the hat buckle to the hat. Attach hat to head band by stapling.

Pilgrim girl hat: Let children color and cut out hat. Staple it to a headband or attach a piece of yarn at each side, so it can be tied under the child's chin.

Native American headband: Let children color and cut out the feathers. They may also decorate the headband and choose several extra feathers to attach to the inside of a headband.

Let children determine where to staple the headbands of the hat they decide to make by bringing the two ends together on their heads, and then paper clipping them. When they take the hats off they may staple them.

Clean Up

Stack patterns for each type of hat together. Throw out any scraps.

Pilgrim Boy Hat

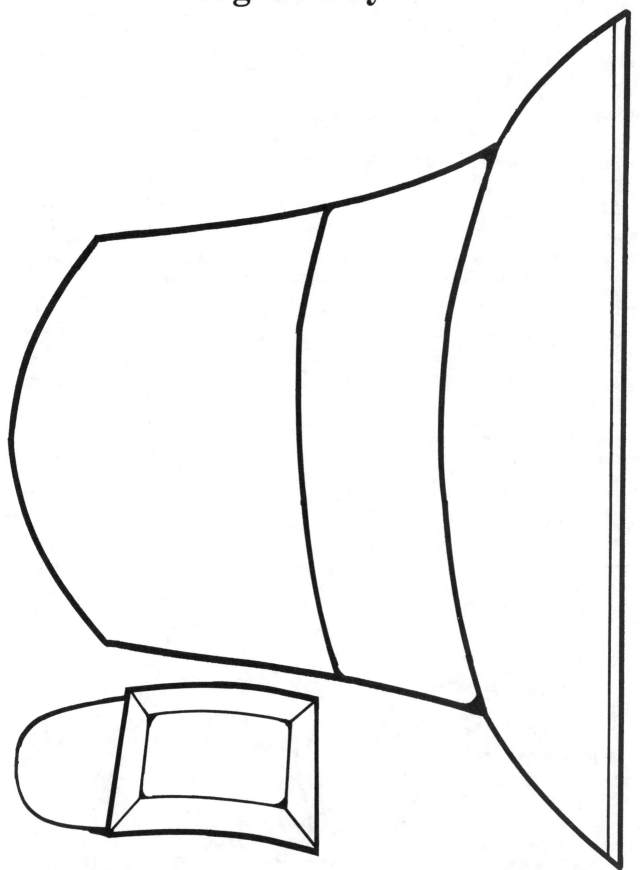

Pilgrim Girl Hat

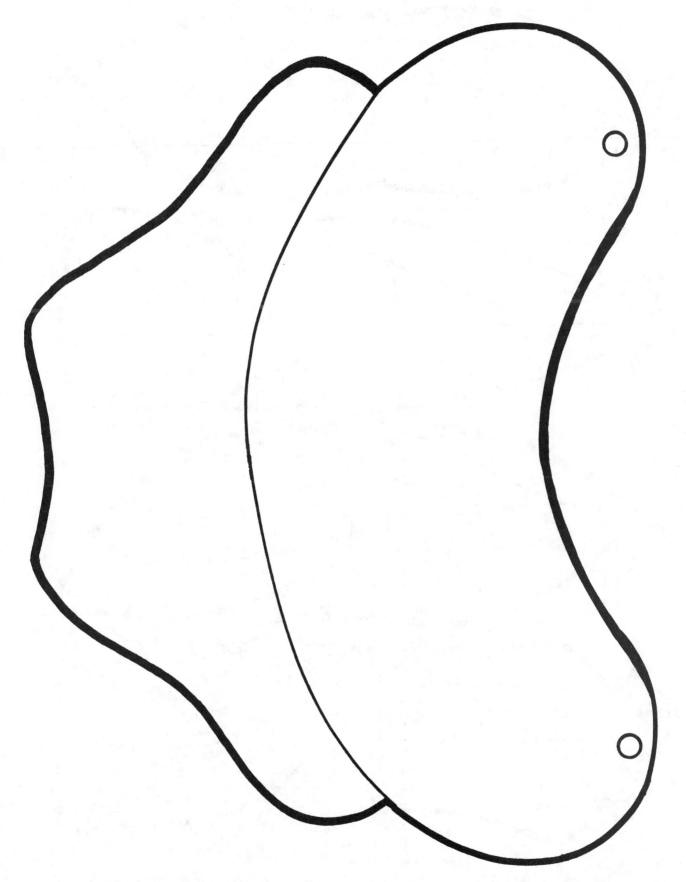

Native American Headband

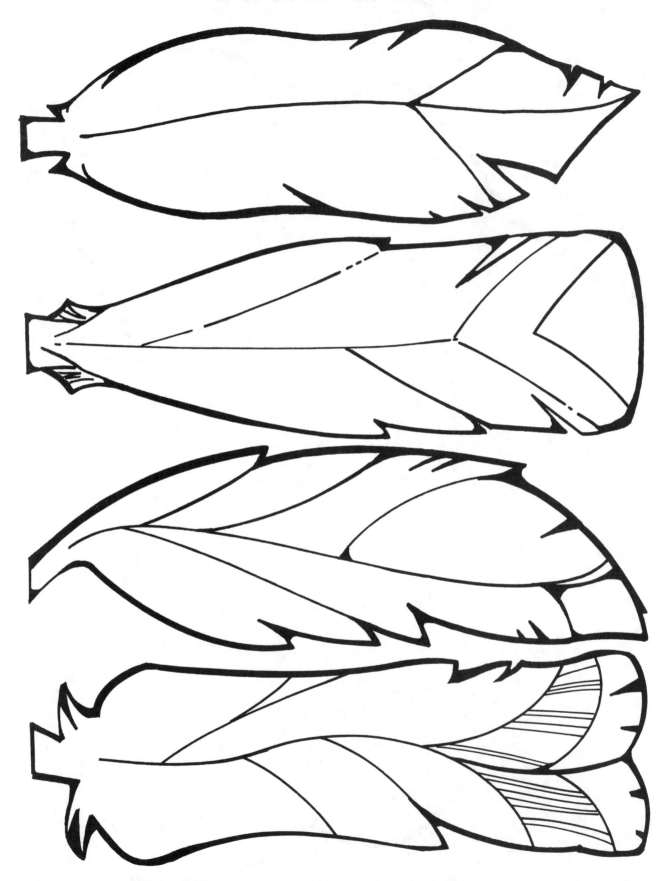

Mosaic Pictures

Purpose

The learner may construct a mosaic to illustrate his/her ideas. These ideas can relate to units of study appropriate to the time of year or to stories that have been read, but they need not be related to any current study in the classroom.

Materials

- Scraps of paper
- Glitter
- Dry cereal
- Feathers
- Beans
- Rice
- Crushed egg shells
- Construction paper
- Glue
- Construction paper
- Small boxes or containers with lids
- Mosaic Picture patterns (pages 134-135)

Preparation

Collect materials needed for mosaics. Sort them into boxes. You may wish to make a mosaic as an example for students to see. Reproduce patterns on pages 134-135 for children to fill in if you wish.

Instructions

Have children take one sheet of colored construction paper and think of a design or picture to create. Using the materials provided they make a mosaic.

Clean Up

Put all materials not used back in boxes and close the lids. Lay the mosaics in a designated area to dry.

Helpful Hints

Send a parent letter home (page 360 or page 361) before organizing this center asking for materials students can use to complete mosaics. Use the completed picture to create a bulletin board display.

Mosaic Picture Pattern

Mosaic Picture Pattern *(cont.)*

Community Helper Stick Puppets

Purpose
Children will cut out, color, and create community helper stick puppets. The child will then tell what each community helper does at his/her job.

Materials
- Community helper patterns (pages 138-139)
- List of community helpers (page 137)
- Oaktag
- Craft sticks
- Glue
- Scissors
- Crayons
- Markers

Preparation
Reproduce the community helper patterns onto oaktag. Reproduce enough so children can have the one they want to work on. Post the list of jobs at the center.

Instructions
Let children color, cut out, attach a community helper to a craft stick. Have them tell or act out the important job each helper does in our community. Have them copy the job title onto the back of the community helper puppet, and then describe what the community helper does.

Clean-Up
Put all supplies away. Have students take community helper stick puppets to their seats.

Community Helpers

Police Officer

A police officer helps people to obey the laws.

Fire Fighter

A fire fighter helps to put out fires.

Librarian

A librarian helps people choose books they will enjoy.

Postal Worker

A postal worker helps mail get places.

Telephone Repairperson

A telephone repairperson helps make sure that telephones are working.

Doctor/Nurse

A doctor or a nurse helps to make people who are sick feel better and prevents others from becoming sick.

Veterinarian

A veterinarian helps sick animals by taking care of them.

House Painter

A house painter helps by painting houses and making them look nice.

Barber/Beautician

A barber or a beautician helps people by cutting and fixing their hair.

Life Guard

A life guard helps by watching people swim and making sure they are safe.

Community Helper Patterns

Community Helper Patterns *(cont.)*

Community Helper Match

Purpose

Given a set of community helpers, the child can match an object identified with the given community helper.

Materials

- Community helper patterns (pages 138-139)
- Community helper stands (pages 141-142)
- Oaktag
- Storage envelopes

Preparation

Run a set of community helpers and stands on oaktag. Color, laminate, and cut out. Slit the double line on each stand. On the back of both the object and stand, write the helper's title. Fold the stands over. Label one envelope Community Helpers and the other Stands for Community Helpers.

Instructions

Have children match each community helper to the correct stand. Have them turn over each object to check to see if they have accurately matched the helpers with their stands.

Clean-Up

Put helpers and objects into the correct envelopes.

Helpful Hints

Children may use the community helper stick puppets they made in the previous center if they wish.

Community Helper Stands

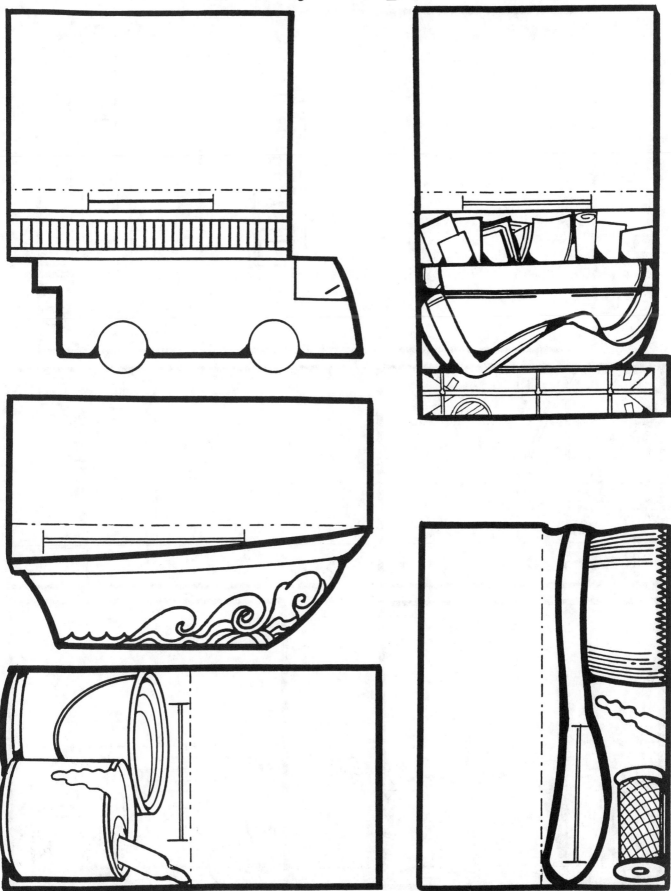

Community Helper Stands (cont.)

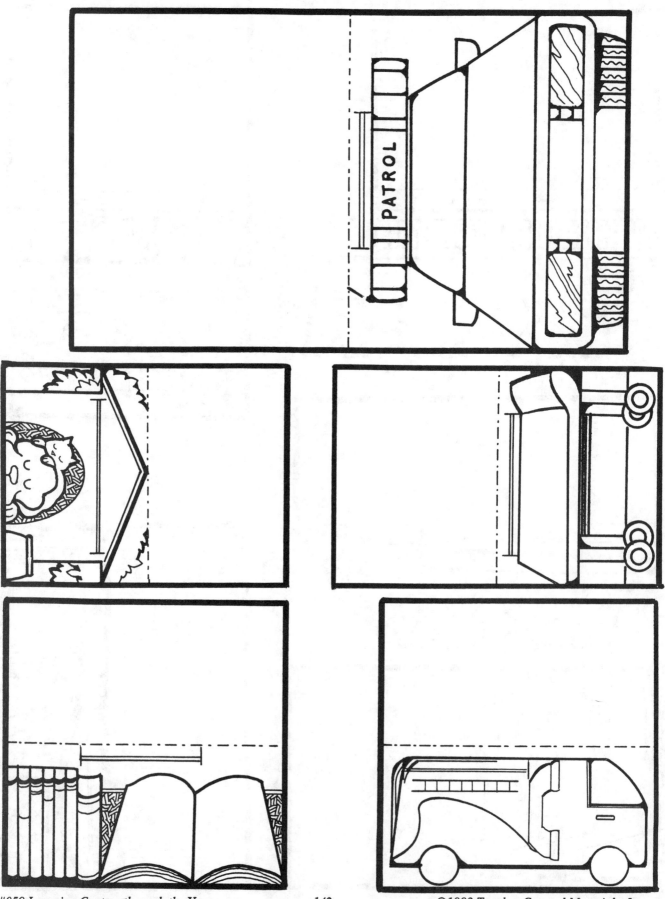

I'm Thankful...

Purpose

Given a little book with four pages the learners can write out and illustrate four things for which they are thankful.

Materials

- Little books (page 144)
- Construction paper
- Scissors
- Stapler
- Pencils
- Crayons

Preparation

Prepare enough little books for each child who uses the center. Cut out construction paper covers for each small book.

Instructions

Have children take a small booklet and write their names and I'm Thankful... on the front of it. They think of four things they are thankful for and write one on each page and illustrate. Let them read the booklets to themselves and be prepared to share their I'm Thankful books with the class.

Clean-Up

Stack any remaining booklets neatly for the next student to use.

I'm Thankful _for food we eat._

I'm Thankful _____

I'm Thankful...
Little Book

I'm Thankful _____

_____

I'm Thankful _____

_____

I'm Thankful _____

_____

I'm Thankful _____

_____

Writing in Shaving Cream

Purpose

Through tactile movement, children will write and form numerals and letters correctly, using shaving cream on a pizza pan.

Materials

- Pizza pan
- Shaving cream

Preparation

Shake can of shaving cream before placing at the center. Newspaper or butcher paper on the table for easy clean up is recommended.

Instructions

Give children very specific instructions on using this shaving cream. Caution them not to put shaving cream in their mouths or eyes. They should spray enough shaving cream to cover the palm of their hand and then wipe their hand on the pizza pan to cover it. Using an index finger on the hand they write with, they can practice forming the numerals 0-9 and the letters A-Z.

Clean Up

Students should take the pizza pan to the sink and wash their hands first, then the pizza pan, using paper towels to dry it off. Return the pan to the table and place the can of shaving cream on top.

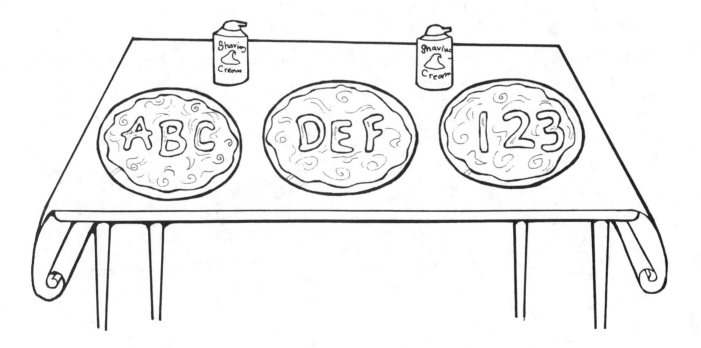

Name Puzzles

Purpose

Children will learn to recognize and read the names of their classmates by putting together a name puzzle for each person in the class.

Materials

- Resealable sandwich bags (one per student)
- Unlined index cards (one per student)
- Storage box
- Scissors

Preparation

In order to make this game, the teacher must write the name of each student on an index card with a marker. Then take scissors and cut up each card into puzzle pieces. Put each name puzzle into a separate bag. Store all bags in a box labelled, "Name Puzzles."

Instructions

Have students take out only one bag at a time so puzzle pieces don't get mixed up. Have students put puzzles together to form a classmate's name, the teacher's name, or their own names. Have them do one puzzle at a time, completing as many puzzles as possible.

Clean-Up

Put all puzzle pieces back in the appropriate bag. Place all puzzle bags in the storage box.

Helpful Hints

This center could be modified and used for different concepts. The puzzles could be made for sight words, number words, color words, or spelling words.

The puzzle pattern on page 147 can be reproduced onto index paper to simplify puzzle making.

Puzzle Pattern

Clothespin Games

Purpose
Children will recognize a color word written on a clothespin and clip it to a card with a picture of a balloon or a hat of that color.

Materials
- Clothespins
- Markers or crayons
- 2 color word games (pages 149-150)
- 2 storage bags

Preparation
Reproduce the clothespin games onto index paper. Color the hats and balloons the colors you wish your students to learn. Laminate for durability. Write the color words onto the clothespin.

Instructions
The students need to complete both card games. They first take out one card and the clothespins that go with it. Have them look at the color word on each clothespin and clip each clothespin to its matching balloon or hat. You or another student may check the answers.

Clean-Up
Store the clothespins in the storage bags.

Helpful Hints
Create clothespin board games for such skills as recognizing short and long vowels, math facts, synonyms, antonyms, and punctuation.

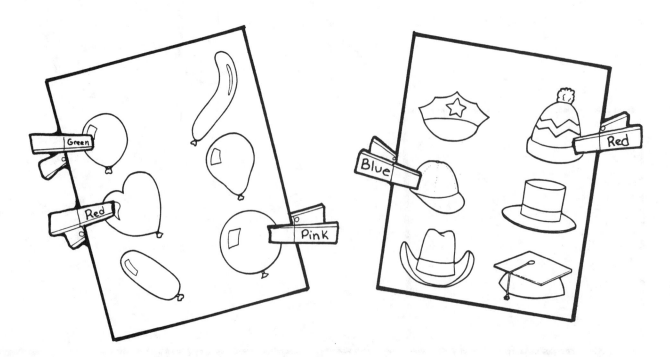

Hat Clothespin Game

Balloon Clothespin Game

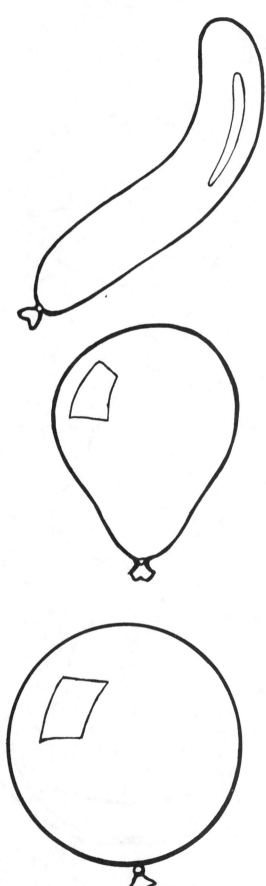

Playing Card Facts

Purpose
Using playing cards, the learner can put the value of cards together to make a given sum.

Materials
- Playing cards
- Envelopes
- Markers

Preparation
Prepare envelopes with a set of playing cards inside. Write the sum of the cards on the outside of each envelope. An envelope pattern is provided on page 152.

Instructions
The student selects an envelope and lays out all the playing cards from inside the envelope. He or she puts two cards together that add up to the sum written on the envelope. Check the answers by looking on the back of the envelopes. Try another envelope.

Clean-Up
Place all cards back into the correct envelope. Children return to seats.

Helpful Hints
Children could also write out the addition facts created by using the playing cards.

Envelope Pattern

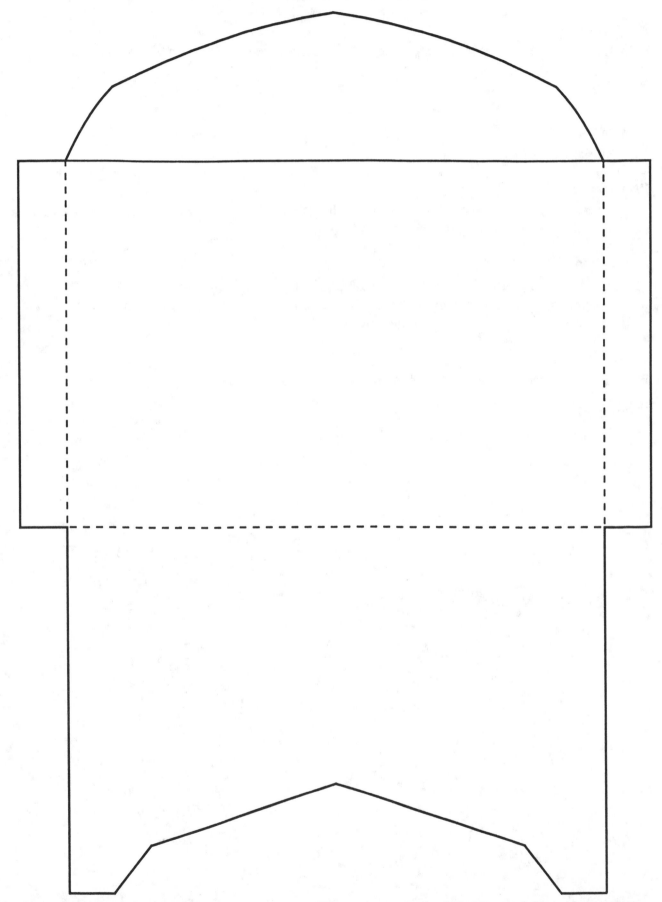

Cover a Sneeze

Purpose

The learner will demonstrate healthy ways to stop the spread of communicable disease.

Materials

- Drawing paper
- Tissues
- Pattern (page 154)
- Crayons
- Scissors
- Glue

Preparation

Reproduce the face pattern. Explain that germs are easily spread and covering a sneeze helps reduce germs.

Instructions

Using the face pattern, students draw their face on it and cut it out. On another paper have them trace their hand and cut it out. Then paste a tissue onto the face and cover it by the hand. Remind them to always remember to cover a sneeze!

Clean-Up

Put everything back.

Helpful Hint

Make a sample project for the center. Remind children to cover a sneeze. Let children make a get well card for any classmate who might be ill. They may use the pattern on page 156 and write a message of their choice inside.

Face Pattern

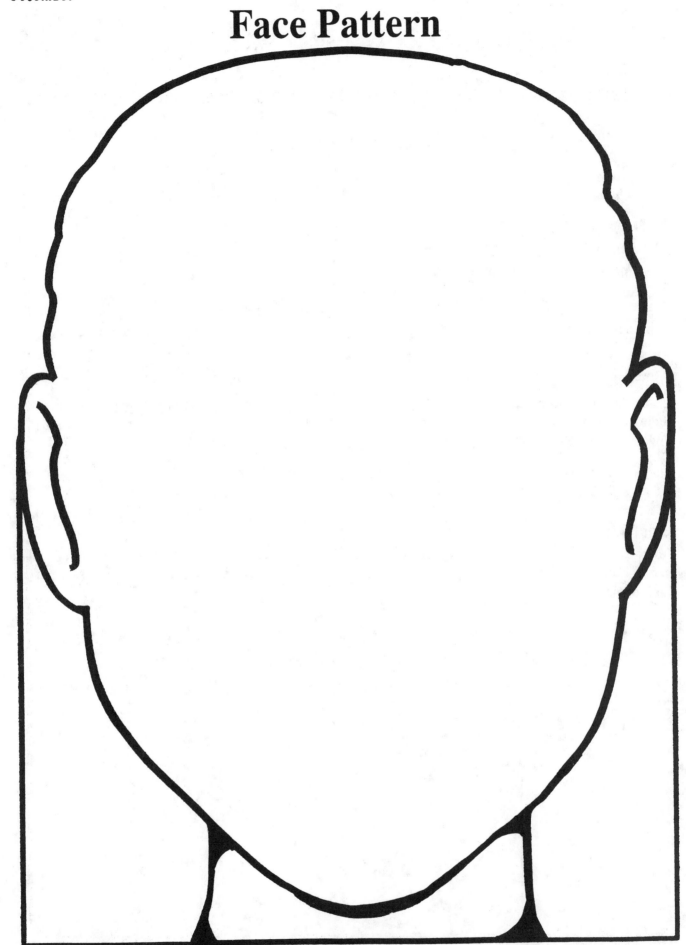

Always Cover a Sneeze!

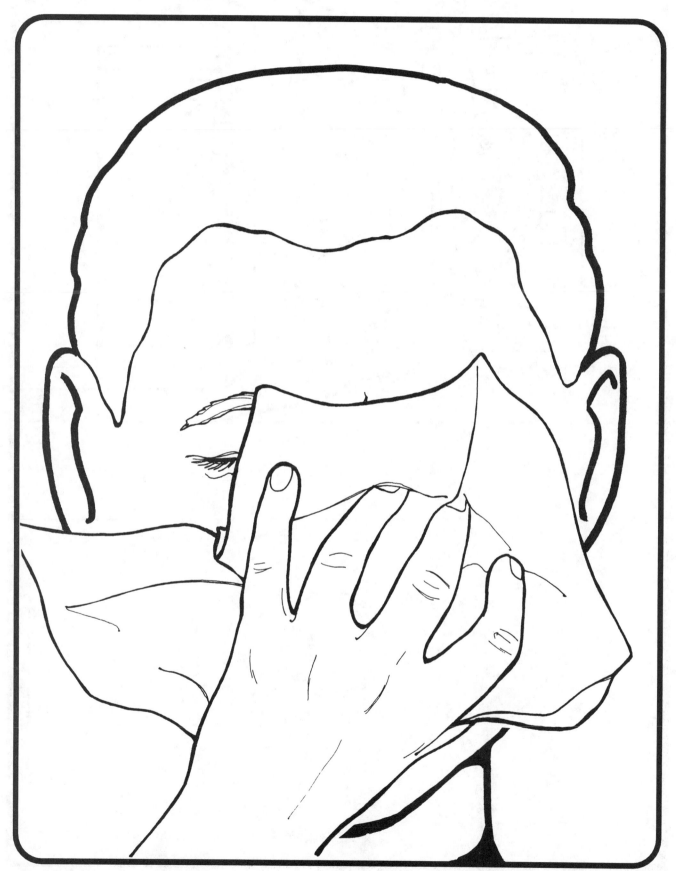

Get Well Card

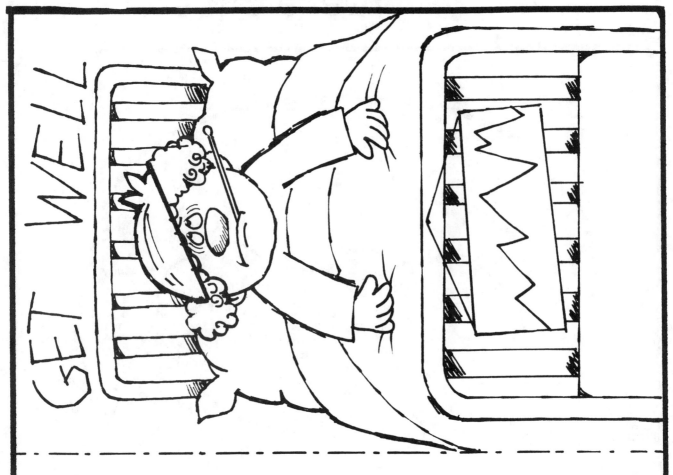

Marshmallow Snowmen

Purpose

Children will use their imaginations to create snowmen from marshmallows.

Materials

- Marshmallows
- Ribbon
- Yarn
- Toothpicks
- Sequins

- Glue
- Paper Punches
- Construction Paper
- Background (page 162)
- Crayons

Preparation

Make sure supplies are available. Be creative with whatever you can provide for the children.
Materials listed are only suggestions. Reproduce for a background.

Instructions

Using available materials, have students create a snowman. Have them make arms with the toothpicks,
a scarf using ribbon or yarns, and use sequins for eyes. They can punch out paper holes for buttons.
Have them color the background and place their snowmen in it.

Clean Up

There are many little pieces to this center. Make sure the scraps are picked up and put away.

Helpful Hints

Reproduce the little book on pages 158-161. Allow the children to finish the pictures and the sentences
and take it home to share.

Little Marshmallow Book

MY MARSHMALLOW BOOK

Written by _____

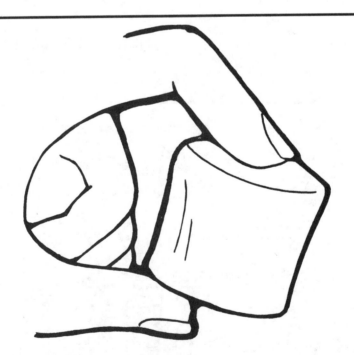

The first time I ate a marshmallow was _____

_____

Little Marshmallow Book *(cont.)*

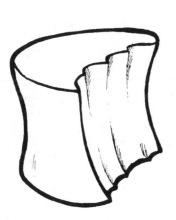

It takes me _____ chews to eat one marshmallow.

A good sandwich would be bread, marshmallows, and _____

_____ .

I think it would taste good to dip a marshmallow into _____ .

Little Marshmallow Book (cont.)

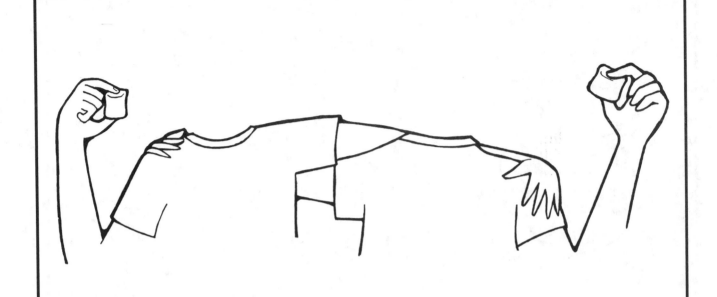

My favorite person to eat a marshmallow with is _____.

My favorite way to eat marshmallows is _____.

Little Marshmallow Book (cont.)

My favorite place to eat marshmallows is _____.

I think a marshmallow looks like _____.

Marshmallow Snowman Background

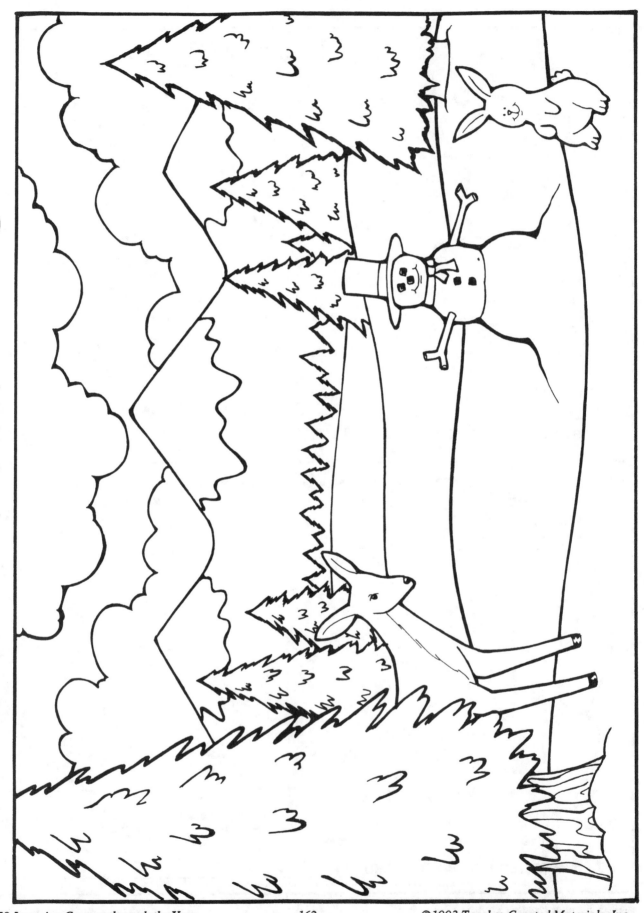

Chalk Drawing

Purpose

Children will create a snowman using white chalk, on blue construction with a missing red mitten placed near the heart.

Materials

- White and colored chalk
- Blue construction paper
- Red construction paper
- Patterns (page 164)

Preparation

If possible, read *The Mystery of the Missing Red Mitten* by Steven Kellogg to the children before they begin working at this center.

Instructions

Have children create a snowman using chalk on the blue construction paper. Give the snowman eyes, a nose, a mouth, a hat, arms, a scarf, and buttons. Have children take a small red mitten and paste it on the snowman as his heart.

Clean Up

Check the chalk as children use it to make sure it is useable for the next student.

Helpful Hints

Use the patterns on page 164. Children may cut them out and add them to the chalk drawing.

Snowman Patterns

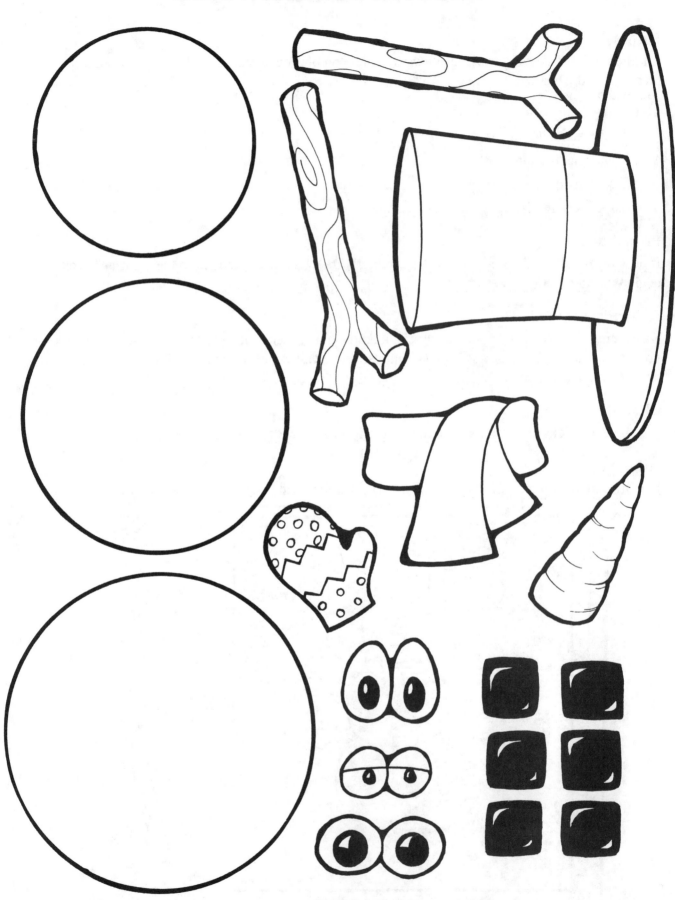

The Lost Mitten Story

Purpose
Children will retell a story about mittens.

Materials
- Story about mittens
- Head set
- Tape recorder
- Blank cassette tapes
- Commercially-prepared or teacher-made stories on tape

Preparation
Purchase a tape of a story about mittens such as *The Missing Red Mitten* by Steven Kellogg or make a tape of a story such as *Caps, Hats, Socks, and Mittens* by Louise Borden (Scholastic, 1989) or the classic rhyme "The Three Little Kittens." (page 168)

Instructions
Have children place the cassette into the tape recorder and put on the headset. Have them locate the first page in the book and follow along as they listen to the story about mittens.

Clean Up
The children should be sure to rewind the tape to the beginning for the next listener.

Helpful Hints
Children can record themselves on tape retelling the story after listening to the recording.

Christmas Crackers

Purpose
After studying the various ways people celebrate Christmas, children will create a Christmas cracker.

Materials
- Gift wrap paper or tissue paper
- Clear tape
- Ribbon or yarn
- Scissors
- Small candies

Preparation
Cut the wrapping paper into 10" x 6" (25 cm x 15cm) sheets. Cut the ribbon or yarn.

Instructions
Overlap ½ inch (1.25 cm) on the two ten inch sides and seal with tape. Slip several small candies in one end and push them toward the middle. Twist each end of the paper and tie the ends at the twisted part. To share crackers, let two children tug at either end, opening the crackers.

Clean Up
If you allow the children to eat the candies in class, have them throw away all wrappers.

Helpful Hints
These crackers were popular in France in the middle 1800's. They are still popular in England, Canada, and Australia.

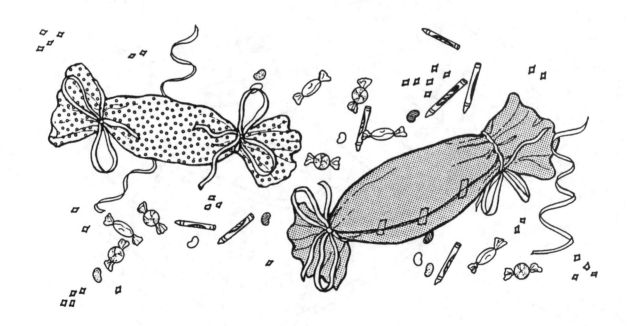

Who Lost a Mitten?

Purpose

Children will brainstorm and create stories about a lost mitten after listening to the story *The Missing Red Mittens* by Steven Kellogg or the rhyme "The Three Little Kittens."

Materials

- Writing paper in mitten shape
- Pencils
- Crayons
- *The Missing Red Mitten* or "The Three Little Kittens" (page 168)
- Mitten Pattern (page 169)
- Story Paper (pages 360-361)

Preparation

Using the pattern, cut writing paper into the shape of a mitten.

Instructions

Have students take a piece of story paper. Have them write their name and finish with the sentence "_____ lost his/her mitten _____." Have them brainstorm an ending and illustrate.

Clean Up

Stack the remaining mitten shaped paper, ready for the next student to use.

Helpful Hints

Read "The Three Little Kittens" to the children and leave a copy at the center.

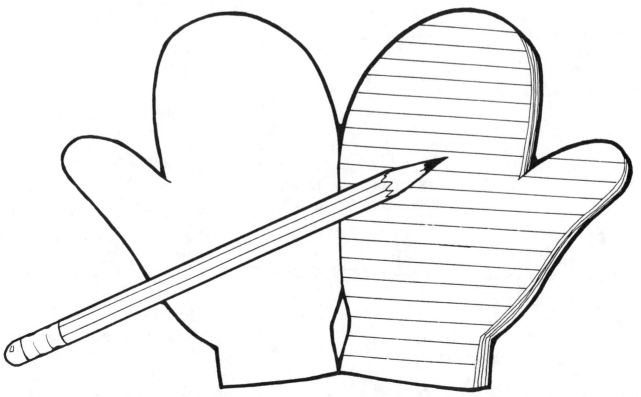

The Three Little Kittens

1

Three little kittens
They lost their mittens
And they began to cry,
"Oh, Mother dear,
We sadly fear
Our mittens we have lost."

2

"What, lost your mittens!
You naughty kittens!
Then you shall have no pie."
Mee-ow, mee-ow, mee-ow.
No, you shall have no pie.

3

The three little kittens
They found their mittens,
and they began to cry,
"Oh, Mother dear,
See here, see here,
For our mittens we have found."

4

"Put on your mittens,
You silly kittens,
And you shall have some pie."
Purr-r, purr-r, purr-r,
Oh, let us have some pie.

5

The three little kittens
Put on their mittens
And so ate up the pie;
"Oh, Mother dear,
We greatly fear
That our mittens we have soiled."

6

"What, soiled your mittens!
You naughty kittens!"
Then they began to sigh.
Mee-ow,mee-ow, mee-ow.
Then they began to sigh.

7

The three little kittens
They washed their mittens
and hung them out to dry;
"Oh, Mother dear,
Do you not hear
our mittens that we have washed?

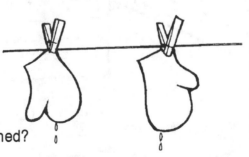

8

"What, washed your mittens!
Then you're good kittens,
But I smell a rat close by."
Mee-ow, mee-ow, mee-ow.
We smell a rat close by.

Mitten Pattern

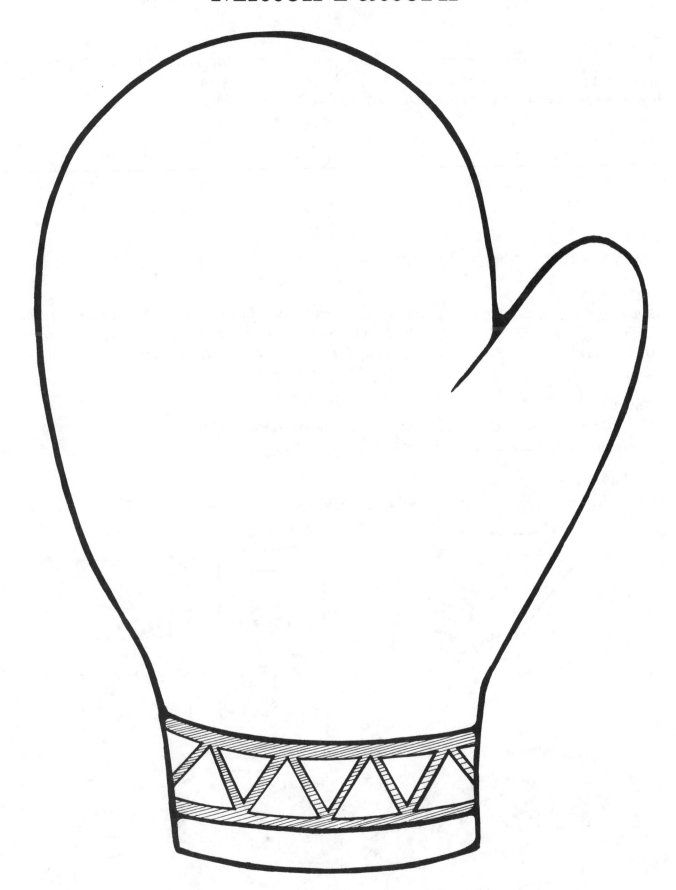

Finger Paint on Paper Plates

Purpose

The learners will improve their fine motor abilities by writing letters and numerals in finger paint on a large paper plate. Writing in finger paint will help the child see the letters and numerals. Using fingers in paint also helps the learner to feel the formation of each letter and numeral.

Materials

- Large white paper plates
- A spoon
- Finger paints

Preparation

Display all supplies for the children to use.

Instructions

Give each child one paper plate. Children are to place one spoonful of finger paint on the plate. Using their writing hand index finger, they form all letters and numbers 1 - 10 on the surface of the plate. After writing letters and numerals, the remaining time can be spent writing words or drawing in the paint.

Clean Up

Have children fold paper plates before throwing them away. Close the finger paint container, wash the spoon and their hands. Place the spoon near the paint container.

Helpful Hints

This center can be adapted to writing spelling words or math problems in finger paints.

Mystery Match

Purpose

Children will practice learning a set of reading vocabulary words by playing a memory matching game with a partner.

Materials

- 3" x 5" (8cm x 13cm) index cards
- Pencils
- A list of words in sets of five on a chart
- Chart for Word Bank (page 172)

Preparation

Prepare a chart with vocabulary words you want your students to know. Use the outline to write your word bank.

Instructions

Each child should take five index cards and a pencil. Together, select from the chart the set of vocabulary words you are going to use. Each player writes one word and definition on another card, then writes his/her name or initials on each card. One child shuffles the ten cards and lays all ten cards face down on the table. Children take turns turning over two cards at a time. If the cards match, the player takes the cards and goes again. If they do not match, the other player goes. Play continues until all matches have been picked up. Each card is read as it is turned over.

Clean Up

Take your five index cards to your seat.

Helpful Hints

Create word banks for any topic you are teaching. Children can play the game as a memory game.

Word Bank Outline

Compound Mittens

Purpose

Children will form compound words by matching pairs of mittens.

Materials

- Several pairs of mittens on colored oaktag (page 174)
- Storage envelope

Preparation

Children can help in the creation of this game. First, brainstorm a list of compound words on the board. Then give each child a pair of mittens to decorate as a matching pair. With a black marker, write the words on the mittens.

Instructions

Let students take the envelope of mittens to the floor where there is adequate space for playing this game. Lay all of the mittens on the floor. Match two mittens together to make a compound word. For example, the word cup printed on one mitten would make a match with a mitten with the word cake. After matching all the mittens, check your compound words.

Clean-Up

Put all mittens in the envelope provided. Return the envelope to the center table.

Mitten Pairs

174

Bean Game

Purpose
The children will sort the beans by color and match the number of yellow and white beans to a fact written on a prepared sheet.

Materials
- Yellow spray paint
- Bag of lima beans
- Newspaper
- Film container
- 8 ½" x 11" (22cm x 28cm) yellow construction paper
- 8 ½" x 11" (22cm x 28cm) white paper
- Markers or crayons

Preparation
To prepare for this center, take a large bag of lima beans and lay them on a piece of newspaper. Using yellow spray paint, paint one side of the beans. Then let them dry. Place 12 beans in a film container.

To make the mat, use an 8 ½" x 11" piece of yellow construction paper and cover half of it with a piece of white paper. List the facts for 12 on an additional sheet and have crayons or markers available at the center.

Instructions
Children will shake the beans in the film container. They will open the lid and spill them onto the yellow and white mat and sort them by color onto the yellow or white side of the mat. For example, there were 12 beans in the container, and a child rolls 4 white and 8 yellow. This demonstrates the fact that 4 + 8 = 12. They should circle this fact on the sheet. Let them roll and spill the beans to get all the facts for 12.

Clean-Up
Put all the beans in the film container. Set all materials on the center table.

Helpful Hints
Children working at this center must be taught to read the beans on the mat from left to right. The left side of the mat should be yellow and the right side white. Therefore, the child would read the yellow number of beans as the first number in the fact sentence. Also the number of beans placed in the film container will depend on the fact family you are presenting or reviewing. Prepare a separate sheet for each fact family.

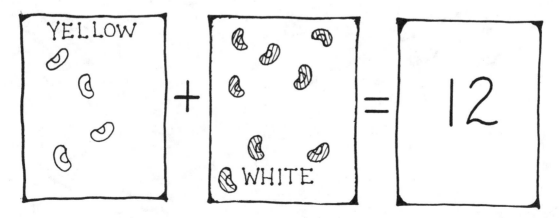

The Planets

Purpose

Using paper, children will create a project using the planets.

Materials

- Crayons
- Variety of colors of paper
- Black construction paper
- White paint and a marble
- Scissors
- Glue
- Box lid
- Planet patterns (page 177)

Preparation

Reproduce the planets. Complete a sample project for display at the center.

Instructions

Give children a large sheet of black construction paper. Using different colors of paper, they cut out the sun and the nine planets in the solar system and paste them onto the black paper. They then place the picture into the bottom of the box lid. Place white paint onto a marble and drop it onto the picture. Move the lid around, causing the marble to roll across the model.

Helpful Hints

Place a chart of the solar system or a sample of the completed project at this center so the children have an example. A jelly roll pan will work in place of the box lid.

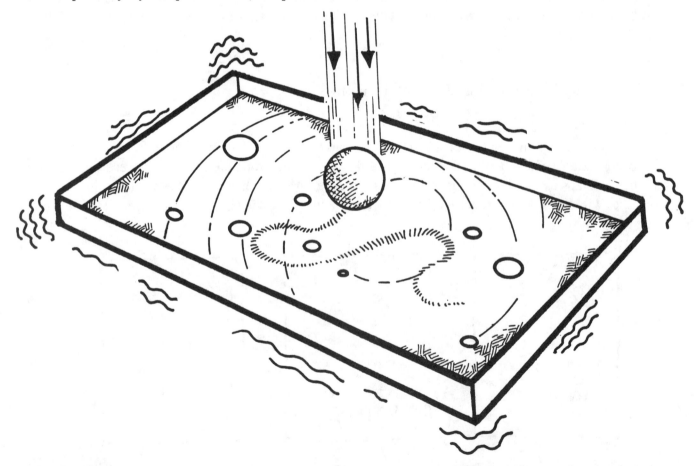

Planet Patterns

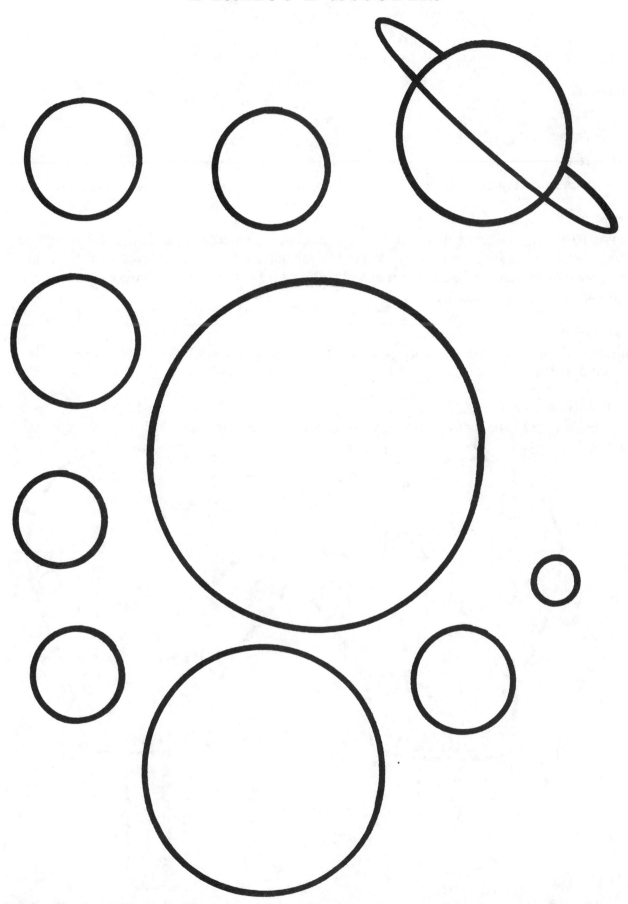

Mitten Poke Hole Activities

Purpose
Children will review a variety of skills by completing the mitten activities.

Materials
- Oaktag
- Hole punch
- Marker
- Mitten Pattern (page 169)

Preparation
Prepare 10-12 large mittens out of oaktag. Then take a hole puncher and punch 10 holes around the mitten. Select a skill for review and create a mitten to reinforce it. Write the problem on the palm of the mitten. Write a choice for an answer at each hole and the correct answer on the back of correct hole that has been poked in the mitten.

Instructions
Children poke a coffee stirrer, golf tee, or pencil tip through the hole with the correct answer. They self-check answers on back.

Helpful Hints
These could be made up for short or long vowels, math facts, or any other skills you want children to practice.

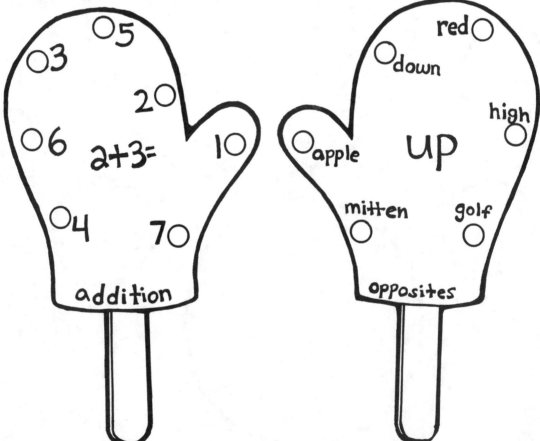

Decorate Mittens

Purpose
Children will create a pair of mittens using a variety of materials.

Materials
- Mittens pattern (page 169)
- Construction paper
- Glue
- Yarn
- Glitter
- Scissors
- Crayons/markers

Preparation
Reproduce the mitten patterns onto oaktag for use as templates.

Instructions
Have children trace and cut out two mittens. Have them decorate the mittens with crayons and glitter. Punch a hole in each of the ends of the mitten. Attach a long piece of yarn and let children wear around their necks.

Clean Up
Put all supplies back into containers. Make sure glitter is cleaned off the table.

Helpful Hints
Children can also take a paper punch, poke holes around the edges, and sew with yarn around the mittens.

Space Creatures

Purpose

Children will create alien or space creature stick puppets and tell a fantasy story about creatures from outer space.

Materials

- Copy of creatures on heavy paper (pages 181-182)
- Crayons/markers
- Glue
- Tongue depressors or craft sticks

Preparation

Reproduce the creatures, onto heavy paper.

Instructions

Have children color the space creatures, and cut them out, then glue them onto a tongue depressors. Encourage students to use their imaginations and develop a story about the creatures.

Clean-Up

Let children take their space creatures back to their seats and share their stories with the whole class.

Space Creature Patterns

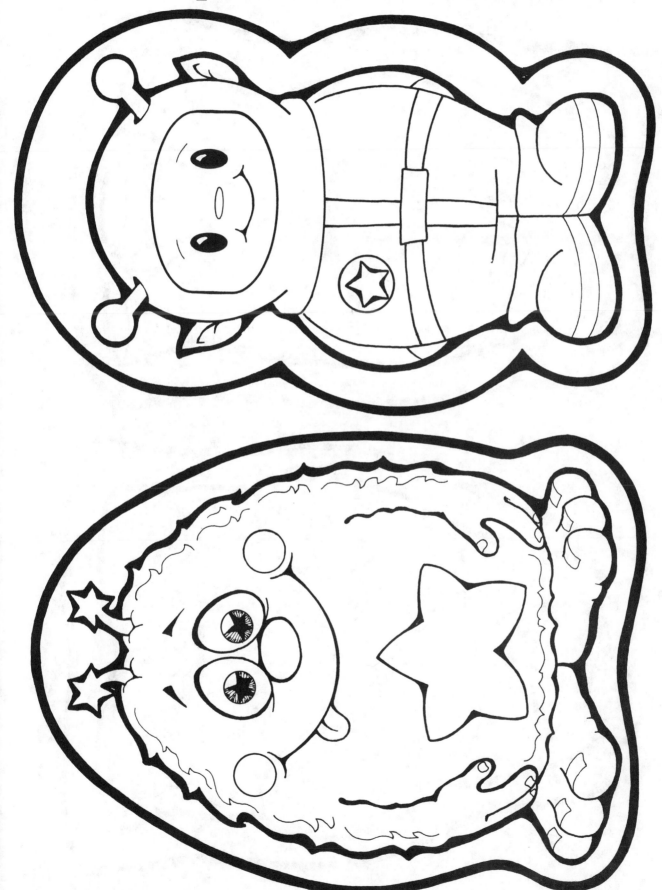

Space Creature Patterns (cont.)

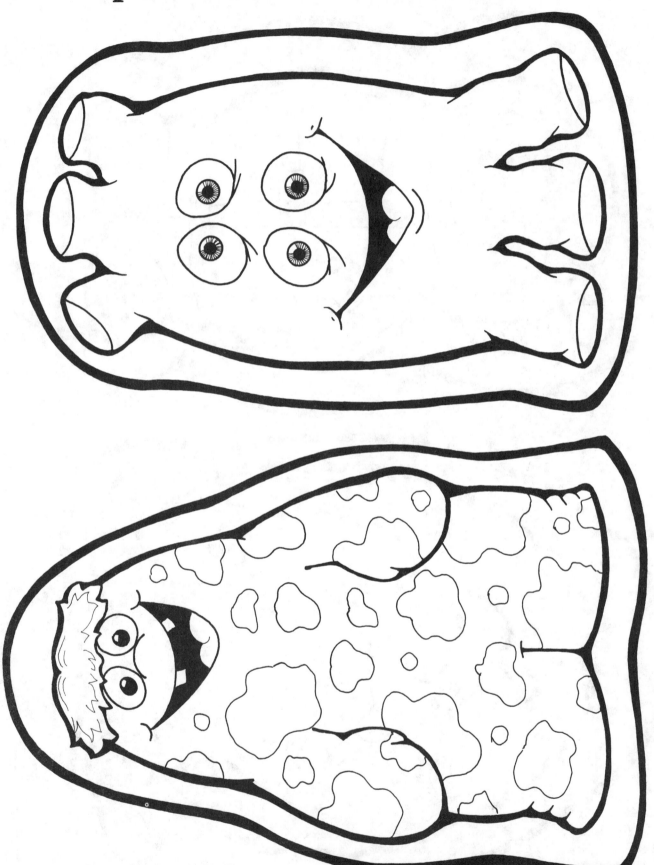

Martin Luther King, Jr.

Purpose

Children will develop their own dream for the picture after hearing books and studying about Martin Luther King, Jr.

Materials

- Martin Luther King, Jr. pattern (page 184)
- Story paper (pages 360-361)
- Pencils
- Scissors
- Construction paper
- Stapler

Preparation

Reproduce the character stencil onto tagboard to create a template. Use it to cut out the story paper. Reproduce the picture to serve as a book cover.

Instructions

On the story paper have children write "I have a dream..." Children finish this open-ended sentence with a dream and a picture they hope the world will be like. They staple their stories together into a booklet with the picture of Martin Luther King, Jr. as the cover.

Clean Up

Children should take their booklets back to their desks and be prepared to share books with a classmate.

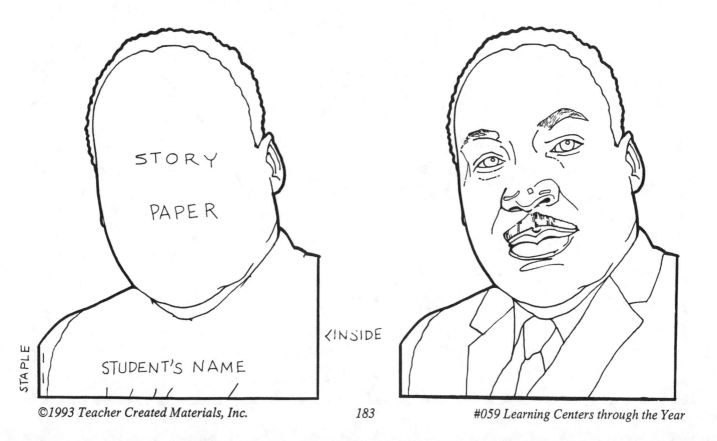

STORY

PAPER

STAPLE

STUDENT'S NAME

<INSIDE

Martin Luther King, Jr. Pattern

A Journey into Space

Purpose
Children will write a story about a journey into space. The story could be a fantasy or based on fact.

Materials
- Writing Paper
- Pencils
- Rocket pattern (page 186)

Preparation
Use the pattern as a template for story paper or as a book cover. Prepare booklets for children to use.

Instructions
Children write a story about a journey they took into outer space. Encourage them to be as imaginative as possible in writing their story. The story may be realistic or a fantasy.

Clean Up
Put away all paper, pencils, and story covers.

Helpful Hints
The story could be written after hearing a reading of *The Magic School Bus: Lost in the Solar System* by Joanna Cole.

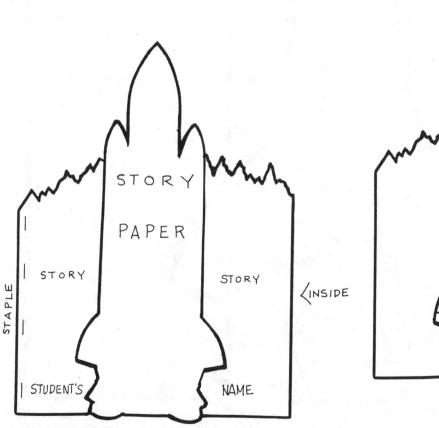

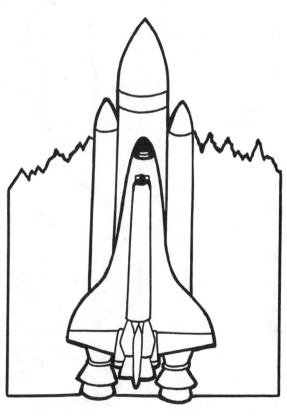

A Journey into Space

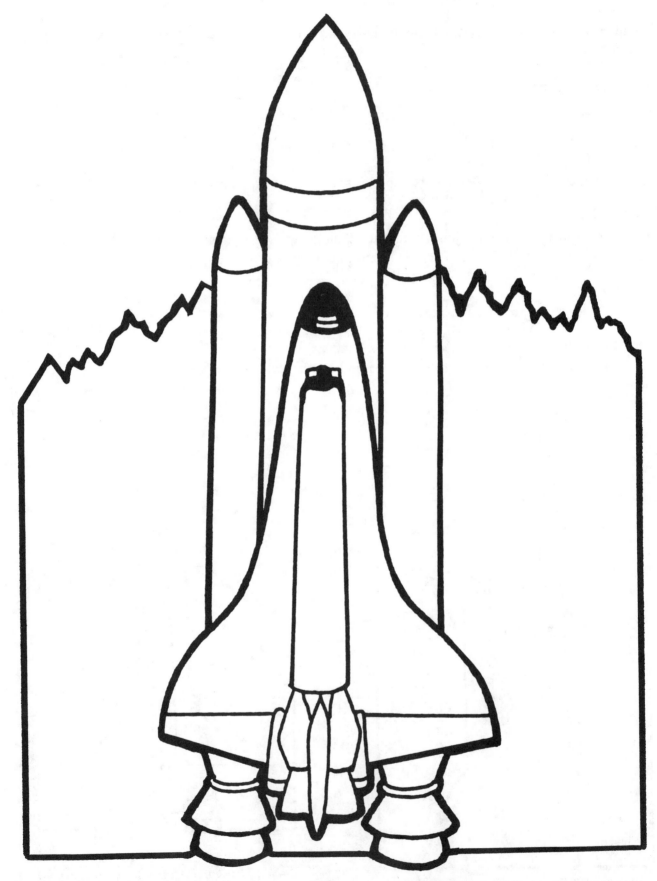

Noodle Necklaces

Purpose

Children will develop their fine-motor abilities by stringing colored noodles on yarn. The children will also develop a sense of patterning.

Materials

- Variety of noodles in different sizes, shapes, and colors. (All noodles must have holes large enough for small hands to put a piece of yarn through.)
- Storage container
- Yarn of various colors
- Food coloring
- 4 cups
- Rubbing alcohol
- Paper toweling

Preparation

Precut yarn so it will fit around children's necks. To dye noodles set out 4 cups; fill each half-full with rubbing alcohol and several drops of food coloring; add noodles; let them set until they reach the desired color; remove noodles and let them dry on paper towels.

Instructions

Have children take a piece of yarn, string noodles onto the yarn in a pattern. When the necklace is finished, tie the yarn in a knot and slip on the necklace.

Clean-Up

Put away noodles and yarn in their storage containers.

Helpful Hints

Examples of noodle necklaces with a pattern displayed at the center may be helpful for children. See page 188 for some ideas. Also, young children will have to be taught how to tie a knot. Select children to help tie knots for the noodle necklace center.

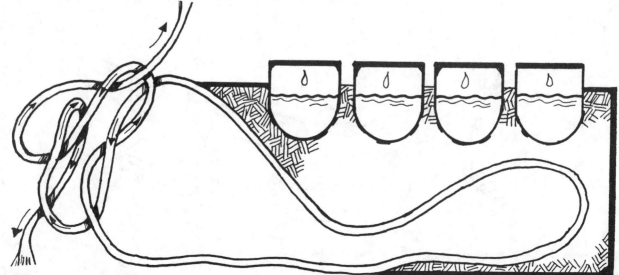

Noodle Necklaces

Noodle Necklace Patterns

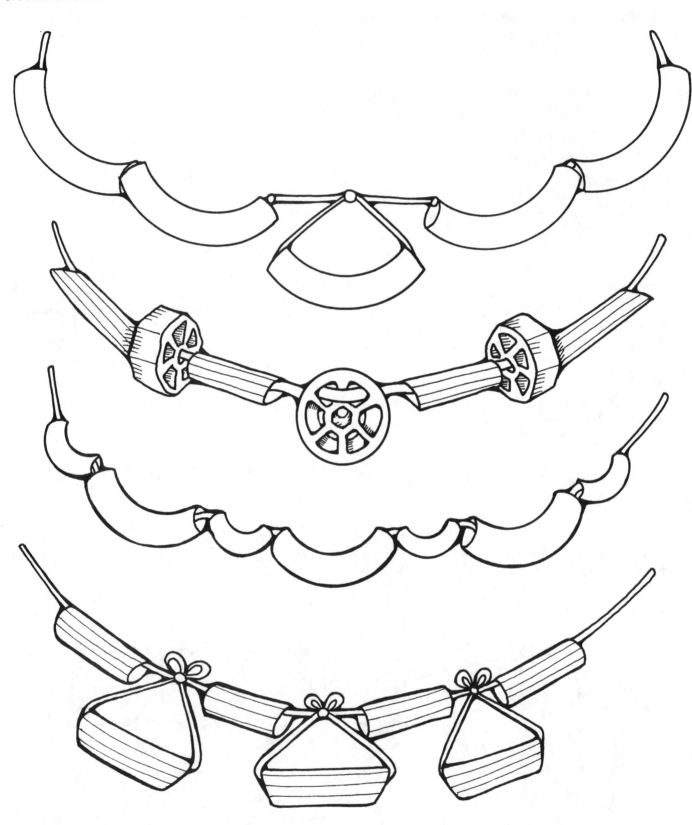

Alphabet Soup

Purpose

Children will arrange several letters in alphabetical order.

Preparation

- Alphabet circles (pages 190-191)
- Soup ladle
- Soup pot

Preparation

Reproduce the alphabet circles onto heavy paper. Place all the letters in a large pot.

Instructions

Using the soup ladle, have children ladle out some letters. Have them lay them out on a table and then arrange them in alphabetical order. Let them put the chips back in the pot, and ladle out more.

Clean-Up

Put all the letters back into the pot and mix them up thoroughly.

Helpful Hints

As an extension, use the words on page 192 and let children try to alphabetize them.

Alphabet Soup

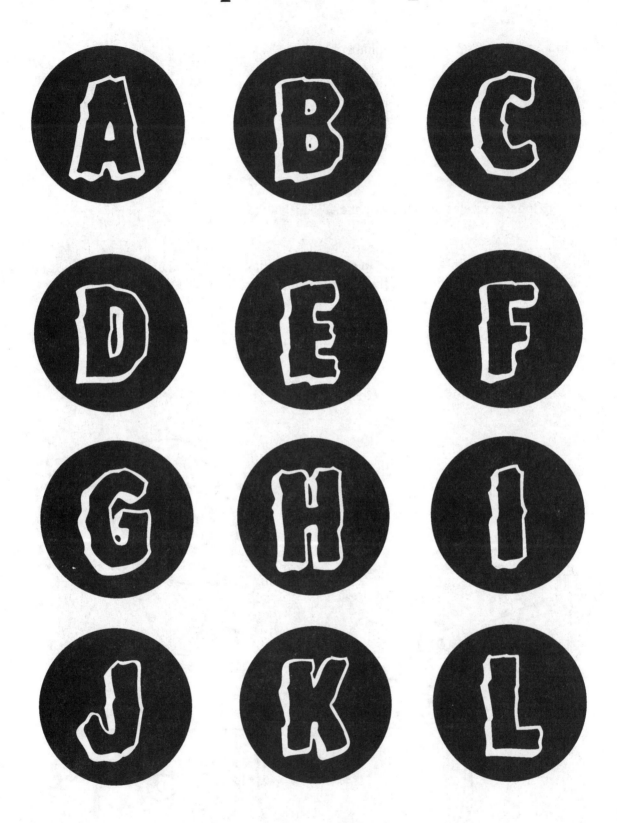

Alphabet Soup (cont.)

Alphabet Soup *(cont.)*

WATER

BREAD

CARROTS

NOODLES

VEGETABLES

SPOON

LADLE

POT

MEAT

TOMATO

ONION

SIMMER

Ordinal Valentines

Purpose

The learner will match the ordinal words first through tenth to their ordinal number 1st - 10th.

Materials

- Hearts (pages 194-195)
- Tagboard
- Paper clips
- Marker
- Index cards 3" x 5" (8cm x 13cm)

Preparation

To make this center, glue ten colored hearts onto a piece of tagboard. Under each heart cut two slits approximately 3" apart and insert paper clips. Label two sets of 3" x 5" index cards with the ordinal words and numbers. Put them into two labeled envelopes.

Instructions

Have children take the two sets of cards out of their envelope. Using the colored hearts on tagboard, clip the ordinal words and numbers under the appropriate heart. Start at the left and work to the right. When children complete the task, either the teacher or a peer should evaluate the work.

Clean-Up

Take the hearts off and put them back into the appropriate envelope.

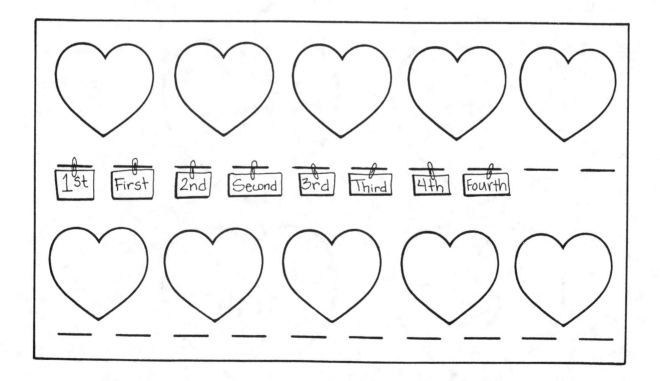

Ordinal Valentines

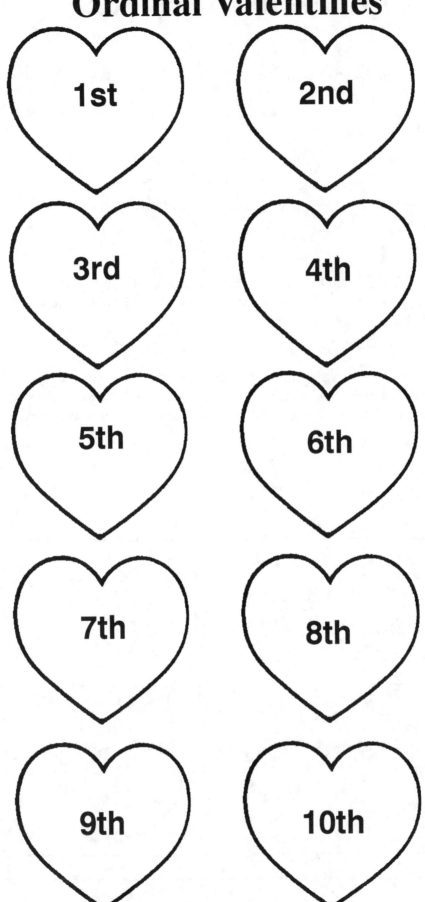

Ordinal Valentines

first

second

third

fourth

h

sixth

nth

eighth

ninth

tenth

DATE ____ TEACHER ____

b. Present ____

b. Absent ____

Total Enrollment ____

Absentees:

*PLEASE LIST ALL STUDENTS WHO ARE ABSENT.
RETURN TO OFFICE DAILY BEFORE 8:45

Broken Heart Facts

Purpose
Children will match one half of a heart with an addition or subtraction fact written on it to the other part of the heart that has the answer written on it.

Materials
- Red and pink hearts (page 205)
- Basket for storage

Preparation
Cut out 20-25 red and pink hearts. Cut them in half. Store in a basket.

Instructions
Have children take the basket of facts to an open space on the floor. Have them lay out all of the broken hearts. Match the half with a fact to the half with the correct answer. Explain to the children they will mend the broken hearts by putting the facts together.

Clean-Up
After work is checked by teacher, put all hearts in the basket. Set the basket on the center table.

Helpful Hints
Broken heart facts can be made for a review of the basic facts to ten, or they can be made as an introductory game to the facts 11-18.

Dental Health

Purpose
Children will identify things that keep teeth healthy and strong.

Materials
- Sentence Strips (page 198)
- Chart paper
- Healthy Tooth (page 199)
- Unhealthy Tooth (page 200)
- Storage envelope

Preparation
Reproduce both the healthy and unhealthy tooth. Use them to create two separate charts. Duplicate the sentence strips onto heavy paper or laminate.

Instructions
Have children remove all sentence strips from the storage envelope and read each sentence. They should decide if the sentence or statement promotes healthy or unhealthy teeth, and lay the strip under the appropriate tooth.

Helpful Hints
On the back of each sentence strip, put the appropriate healthy or unhealthy tooth. Children may then self-check work by turning over each sentence strip and checking for the appropriate tooth.

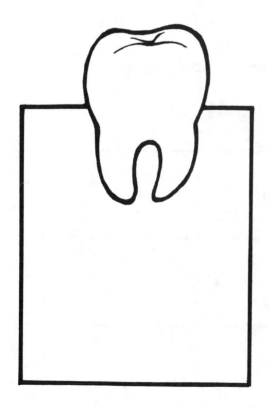
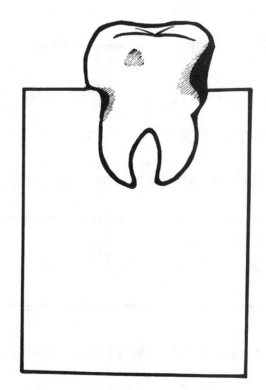

Sentence Strips

Brush your teeth after eating.

Floss your teeth.

Visit your dentist regularly.

Eat healthy foods.

If you chew gum, make sure it is sugarless.

Eat candy.

Open bottles with your teeth.

Chew gum that has sugar.

Brush your teeth once a week.

Do not use dental floss.

Healthy Tooth

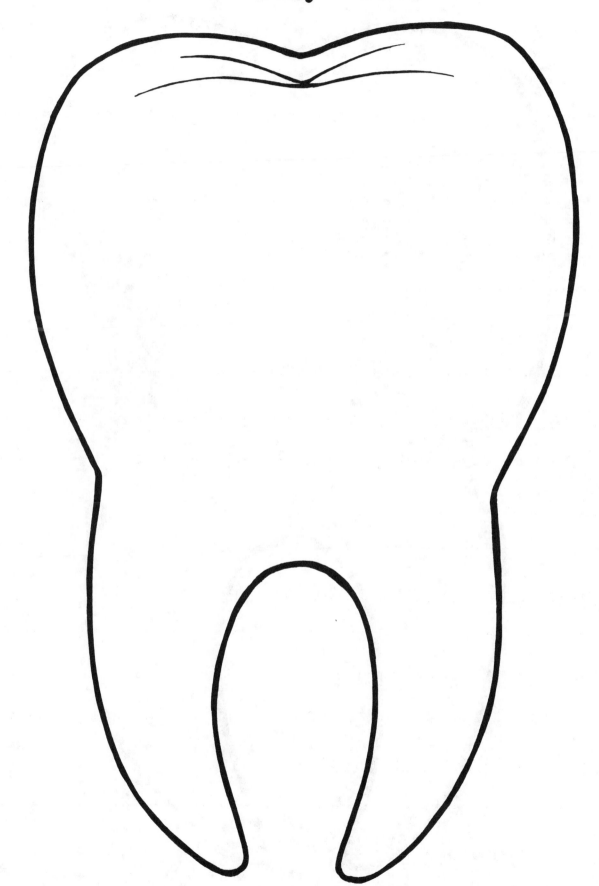

Unhealthy Tooth

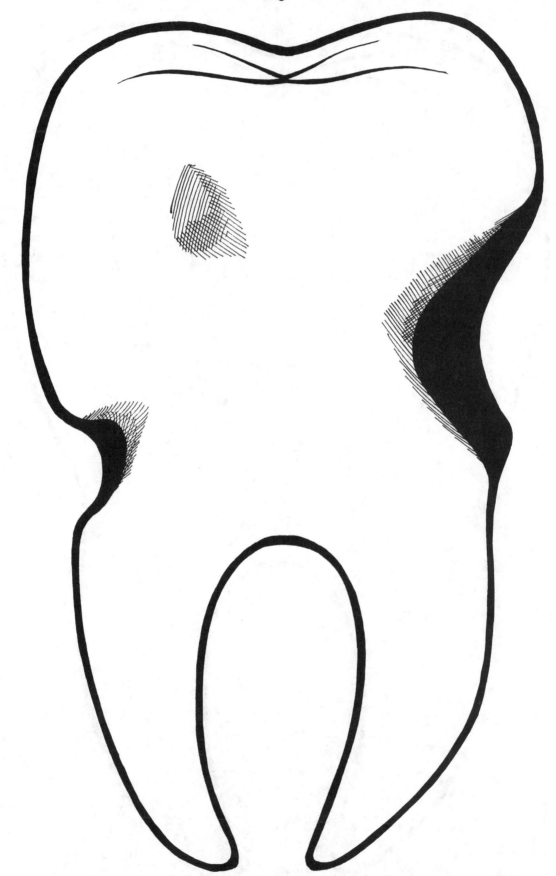

Groundhog

Purpose

Children will make a groundhog puppet for Groundhog Day.

Materials

- Oaktag
- Crayons
- Scissors
- Brown and green construction paper
- Flashlight
- Patterns (pages 202-203)

Preparation

Reproduce the patterns onto oaktag to create templates.

Instructions

Have children trace the groundhog onto brown paper and the hole onto green paper. Cut out and color both. Paste a tongue depressor onto the back of the groundhog. Cut a slit for the groundhog to poke through. Use a flashlight to create a shadow for the groundhog.

Clean Up

Throw away all scraps and then turn off flashlight.

Groundhog Pattern

Groundhog's Hole Pattern

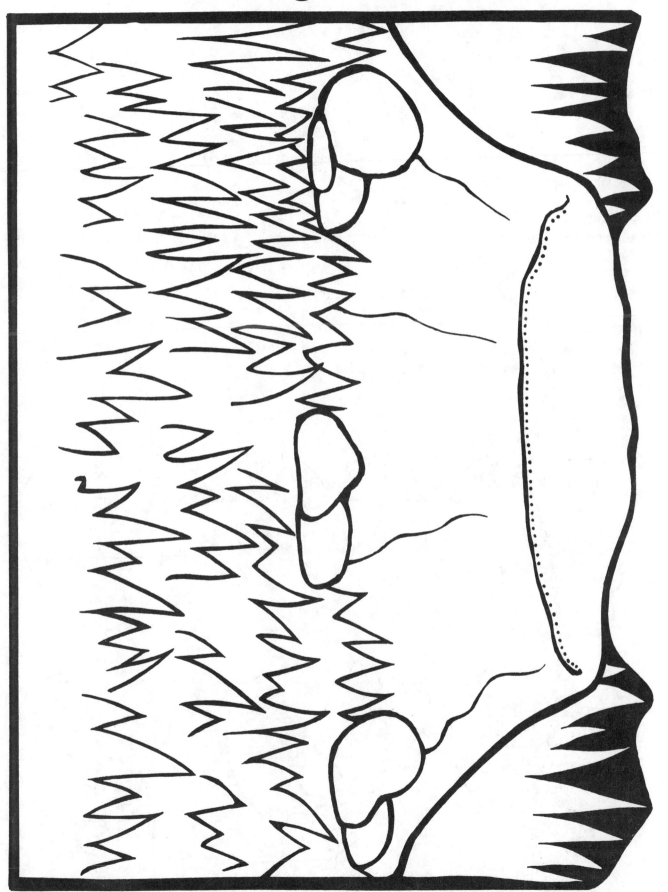

Create a Valentine

Purpose

Children will use the materials provided to make a Valentine heart.

Materials

- Lace
- Red, pink, white paper
- Scissors
- Markers

- Crayons
- Glue
- Patterns (page 205)

Preparation

Make templates out of patterns on page 205. Have materials ready. Encourage creative use of materials.

Instructions

Have children use the materials to create a Valentine for someone special.

Helpful Hints

Children may wish to add Valentine sayings to their heart, such as "Be Mine" or "I Love You". See page 206. These may be copied or cut out and added to the Valentines.

Valentine Patterns

Valentine Sayings

Story Quilt

Purpose

After listening to *The Velveteen Rabbit* and other stories about favorite stuffed toys, each child will make a small piece of a story quilt. The story quilt will illustrate our most lovable stuffed toys.

Materials

- *The Velveteen Rabbit* or books about stuffed toys
- Paste
- Several stuffed animals
- 4"/10 cm white construction paper squares
- Crayons
- Large banner - Our Favorite Stuffed Toys (pages 208-209)

Preparation

Using butcher paper or construction paper taped together, create an outline for children to put their quilt pieces together. At an area accessible to the children, place the quilt outline so children can glue their pieces to it. Use pages 208-209 to make a large banner. Enlarge it if possible. Color it. Display with the finished quilt.

Instructions

Each child takes a quilt piece. On it they draw and color their favorite stuffed toy. When finished, they paste it onto the large quilt in an outlined area.

Clean Up

Put all extra supplies away neatly, and have children attach their quilt piece to the class quilt.

Helpful Hints

Story quilts can be made for any number of stories. They make an attractive bulletin board.

Penny and Quarter

Purpose

Using patterns, children will create large models of a penny and a quarter after learning about Abraham Lincoln and George Washington.

Materials

• Patterns for penny and quarter (pages 211 and 212)

• Scissors

• Tape

Preparation

Reproduce the penny and quarter patterns. Make up a sample of a penny and a quarter for children to see at the center.

Instructions

Have children color and cut out the penny and the quarter. Then paste together a front and back to make a coin.

Clean Up

Stack all the backs and fronts of each coin denomination; keep denominations separate.

Helpful Hints

Real coins may be useful for children to see while working. You might have several displayed.

Penny Pattern

Quarter Pattern

Love Letters

Purpose

Children write a love letter to a special person following guidelines for writing a friendly letter.

Materials

- Friendly letter chart (page 214)
- Paper
- Envelope pattern (page 152)
- Stickers
- Pens and pencils
- Writing paper or stationery (page 215)

Preparation

Prepare the chart for the center; include some stationery for children to use in writing their letters.

Instructions

Have children follow the steps on the chart and write a love letter to someone special. The letter should begin with today's date. The greeting should include the person's name. The body of the letter should include why the person is so special. Make sure children close letters and sign their names. They may make envelopes or use one provided.

Clean Up

Stationery and envelopes should be put back neatly. Make sure there are plenty of writing supplies.

Helpful Hints

Reproduce the stationery for children to use. Ask parents to provide stationery for use at this center. Send home one of the letters on pages 360-361.

Friendly Letter

This is how to write a friendly letter.

Heading: February 14, 19 _____

Greeting: Dear Class,

Body: I am happy to be your teacher. You are very special to me! I love learning about new things with you.

Closing: Love,

Signature: _____

Love Letter Stationery

Love • Kisses • Honey • Sweetums • Hugs • Smoochies •

Kisses

Love

Honey

Love • Kisses • Honey • Sweetums • Hugs • Smoochies •

Bag of Paint

Purpose

The learner will practice writing letters, numbers, and words using bags of paint.

Materials

- Several colors of paint
- $\frac{1}{2}$ gallon resealable bags
- Poster board

Preparation

Fill several half gallon resealable bags with two to three tablespoons (about 40 mL) of red paint. Seal tightly. On the posterboard prepare a large chart of the letters, numbers, or words you would like the children to practice.

Instructions

Take a bag of paint. Lay it on a flat surface. Use your hands to smooth out the paint in the bag. The children use their finger and practice writing letters and numbers.

Clean Up

Seal all bags tightly so no paint leaks out.

Helpful Hints

It helps to have several bags made of ahead of time so, if a bag gets torn, it can be thrown away and another is readily available.

Story Sequencing

Purpose
Children will learn how to put parts of a familiar story in sequence.

Materials
- Three different stories, reproduced (pages 218-220)
- Three different colors construction paper
- Glue
- Envelope or bag

Preparation
Run one copy of three different stories your children have read and enjoyed. You can also use the three stories in this book or others your class has enjoyed. Glue the pages from each story onto three different colors of construction paper. Store each story in a separate envelope or bag. For each story, cut apart the paragraphs. Number them on the back to show the correct sequence.

Instructions
Students select one envelope containing a story. They lay the pieces of the story on the table, and read each paragraph, laying the paragraphs in order by what happens. Once they feel they have put the story in order correctly, turn over the paragraphs. Check to see if the paragraphs were in numerical order.

Clean-Up
Return all parts of the story to the storage envelope.

Helpful Hints
It is best to provide three or more stories for children who use this center frequently.

Sequencing

Goldilocks and the Three Bears

Once upon a time three bears lived in a cottage in the woods. They were Papa Bear, Mama Bear, and Baby Bear.

One morning they decided to take a walk while their porridge was cooling. Soon, Goldilocks came to the bears' cottage. She was lost and hungry. Since no one was home, she went right in.

Goldilocks saw three bowls on the table. She tasted Papa Bear's porridge. It was too hot. She tasted Mama Bear's porridge. It was too cold. She tasted Baby Bear's porridge. It was just right. So, she ate it all up.

Now Goldilocks wanted to rest. She saw three chairs. She sat in the big chair. It was too hard. She sat in the middle-sized chair. It was too soft. She sat in the little chair. It was just right. But, it broke all to pieces.

Goldilocks and the Three Bears *(cont.)*

Goldilocks was very tired. She saw the three beds. She tried the big bed. It was too hard. She tried the middle-sized bed. It was too soft. She tried the little bed. It was just right. So, she fell fast asleep.

The three bears came back. Papa Bear said, "Someone has been eating my porridge." Mama Bear said, "Someone has been eating my porridge." Baby Bear said, "Someone has been eating my porridge. And, they ate it all up!" The bears saw their chairs. Papa Bear said, "Someone has been sitting in my chair." Mama Bear said, "Someone has been sitting in my chair." Baby Bear said, "Someone has been sitting in my chair. And, it is all broken." The three bears saw their beds. Papa Bear said, "Someone has been sleeping in my bed." Mama Bear said, "Someone has been sleeping in my bed." Baby Bear said, "Someone has been sleeping in my bed. And, here she is!" Goldilocks woke up. When she saw the three bears, she jumped out of bed and ran home.

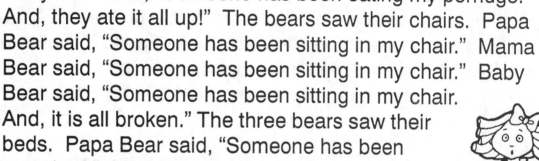

The Three Little Pigs

Once upon a time three little pigs went out to seek their fortunes. The first little pig met a man with a load of straw. "May I have some straw to build a house?" asked the pig. And the man gave him some. The first little pig worked hard to build his straw house. He was happy!

One day a big, bad wolf came by. "Little Pig, Little Pig, let me come in!" "Oh! No! Not by the hair of my chinny chin!" said the pig. So the wolf huffed and he puffed and he blew the house down. The second little pig met a man with a bundle of sticks. "May I have some sticks to build a house?" asked the pig. And the man gave him some. The second little pig worked hard to build his stick house. He was happy!

The Three Little Pigs *(cont.)*

One day a big, bad wolf came by. "Little Pig, Little Pig, let me come in!""Oh! No! Not by the hair of my chinny chin chin!" said the pig. So the wolf huffed and he puffed and he blew the house down. The third little pig met a man with a pile of bricks. "May I have some bricks to build a house?" asked the pig. And the man gave him some. The third little pig worked hard to build his brick house. He was happy!

One day a big, bad wolf came by. "Little Pig, Little Pig, let me come in!" "Oh! No! Not by the hair of my chinny chin chin!" said the pig. So the wolf huffed and he puffed, but he could not blow down the brick house. "Please let me just peek my nose into your door," begged the wolf. But the pig said, "No!" The wolf was mad! He climbed on the roof of the brick house. Then he slid down the chimney. Little Pig had a pot of boiling water on the fire. With a loud splash the wolf fell into the pot. That was the end of the big, bad wolf.

The Three Billy Goats Gruff

Once upon a time there lived three billy goats and the name of all three was Gruff. The three wanted to go up to the hillside to eat grass to make themselves fat. In order to get to the hillside they had to cross a wooden bridge which was over a stream. Under the bridge lived an ugly little troll with enormous eyes and a very, very, long nose.

The first to reach the bridge was the youngest billy goat Gruff. "Trip, trap; trip, trap!" went the bridge. "Who's that trip - trapping over my bridge?" roared the ugly little troll from underneath the bridge. "It's only me, tiny little billy goat Gruff. I'm going to the hillside to eat grass," he said in a tiny little voice. "Oh no you're not!" thundered the troll, "I'm going to come and eat you up." "Oh no, don't eat me. Wait for my brother, the middle billy goat Gruff. He's much fatter than me." "Fatter you say? Then, very well, be on your way." So the youngest billy goat Gruff went trip-trap, trip-trap across the bridge.

The Three Billy Goats Gruff *(cont.)*

A few minutes later the middle billy goat Gruff started over the bridge. "Trip, trap; trip, trap!" went the bridge. "Who's that trip - trapping over my bridge?" roared the ugly little troll from underneath the bridge. "It's only me, medium-sized billy goat Gruff. I'm going to the hillside to eat grass," he said in a medium-sized voice. "Oh no you're not!" thundered the troll, "I'm going to come and eat you up." "Oh no, don't eat me. Wait for my brother, the big billy goat Gruff. He's much fatter than me." "Fatter you say? Then, very well, be on your way."

So the middle billy goat Gruff went trip-trap, trip-trap across the bridge. Quite soon the big billy goat Gruff appeared. "Trip, trap; trip, trap!" went the bridge. "Who's that trip-trapping across my bridge?" roared the ugly little troll from underneath the bridge. "It's only me, big-billy goat Gruff. I'm going to the hillside to eat grass," he said in a big-sized voice. "Oh no you're not!" thundered the troll, "I'm going to come and eat you up." "Come up and try to eat me!" shouted the big billy goat Gruff. And meet my two sharp horns."

The ugly little troll climbed to the top of the bridge, where the big billy goat Gruff charged the troll with his sharp horns, causing him to turn somersaults off the bridge and into the stream. The troll was never seen again. Big billy goat Gruff went trip - trap, trip - trap over the bridge to eat grass on the hillside with his brothers. And there the three billy goats Gruff can be found still, as long as there's grass on the hill!

Cartoon Sequencing

Purpose
By reading and looking at pictures, the learner can put parts of a cartoon into the correct order.

Materials
- Cartoons
- Pencils
- Markers or crayons

Preparation
In preparation for this center the teacher will select and cut out cartoons from the newspaper. These cartoons should be age appropriate, as well as at the reading level of the students. After finding 4-5 cartoons, cut them apart. Number the backs of each section for self-checking. Place each cartoon in a separate bag for storage.

Instructions
Children select a bag containing a cartoon. Lay the pieces on the table. Read the sections and arrange them in order. Turn the parts of the cartoon over and check that the pieces are in numerical order. Complete all the cartoons.

Clean-Up
Always put one cartoon away before beginning another one. Place all parts in the appropriate bag.

Helpful Hints
The teacher could also draw cartoons or use coloring books to create the cartoons for this center. To write your own cartoons, use the blanks on pages 225 and 226.

Cartoon #1

Cartoon #2

Money Eggs

Purpose
Children will practice counting change with pennies, nickels, and dimes by using flash cards.

Materials
- Pastel colored construction paper
- Egg-shaped pattern (page 228)
- Basket with artificial grass
- Paper coins (pages 52, 229-231)

Preparation
Out of pastel colored construction paper, cut ten egg shapes. Glue paper coins onto the egg. Print the total amount of change on the back of each egg. Laminate the eggs, and place in the plastic basket for storage.

Instructions
Children take one egg flash card out of the basket at a time. They are to look at the coins pasted onto the front of the egg and determine how much money it equals. They may then check the back of the egg for the correct answer.

Clean Up
Place all the eggs in the basket for storing.

Helpful Hints
You may wish to extend this activity to using quarters.

Egg-shaped flash cards are easy to make and can be used for drill and practice of other skills.

Egg-Shaped Patterns

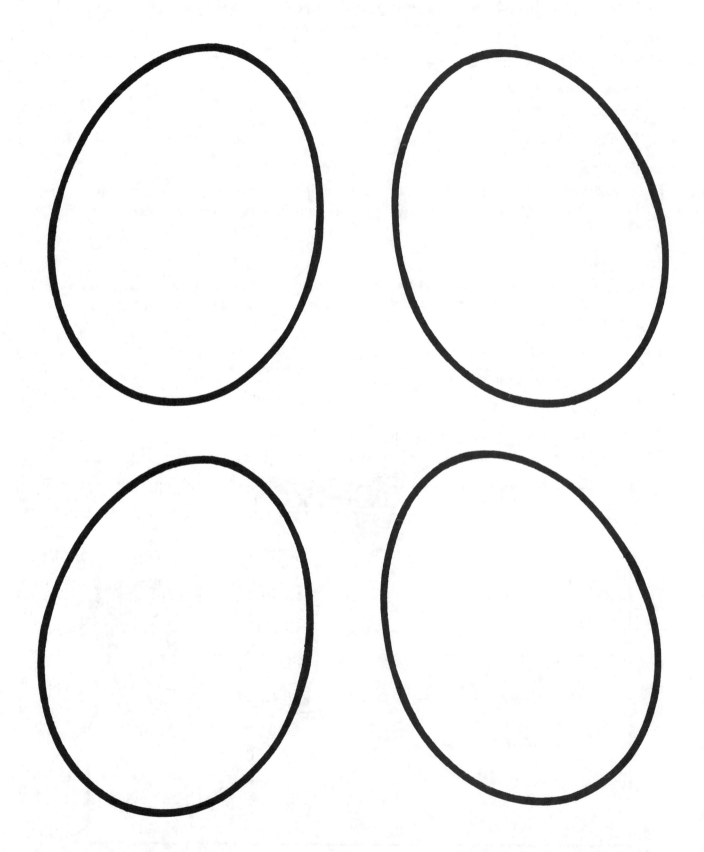

Nickels

Dimes

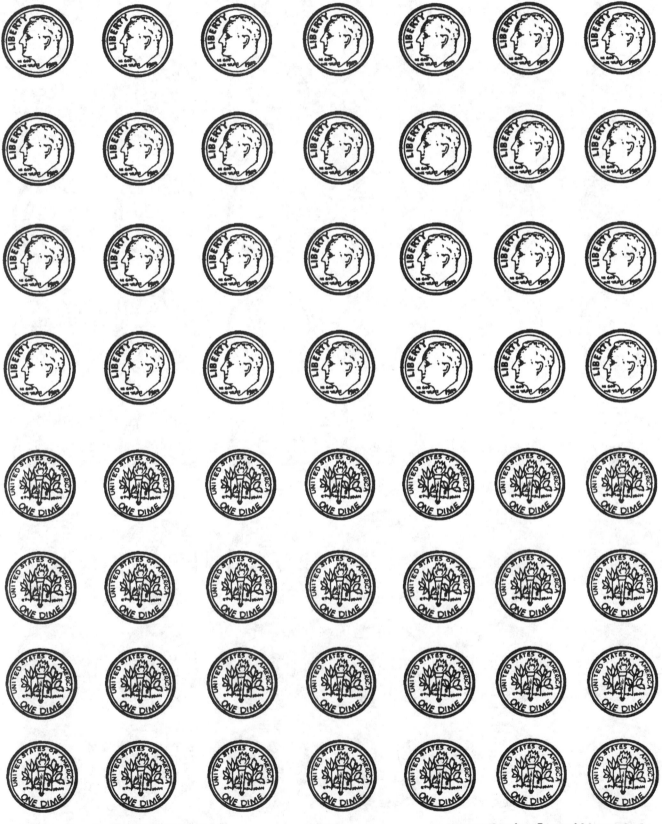

Quarters

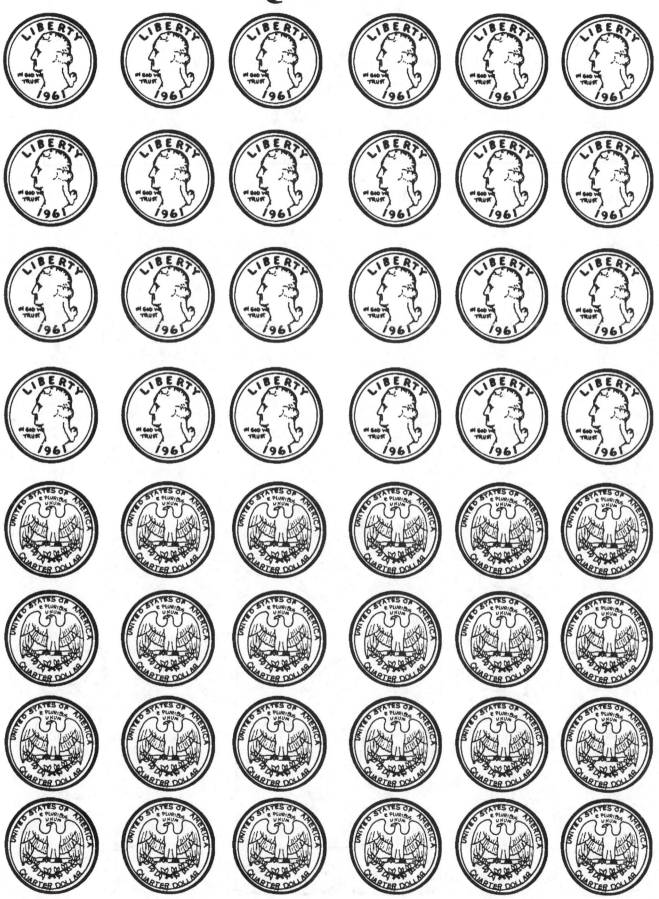

Dress for the Weather

Purpose
Given a set of paper dolls, children will dress the dolls according to the weather.

Materials
- Weather cards (pages 233-236)
- Heavy paper
- Girl and boy paper doll (page 237)
- Doll clothing (pages 238-241)
- Clothing
- Storage envelopes
- File folders

Preparation
Reproduce the paper dolls onto heavy paper. Color, laminate, and cut out. Reproduce the clothing. Color and cut out. Reproduce the weather card backgrounds and color them. Glue them onto file folder to make them stand up.

Instructions
Children select a weather card and a doll. By looking at the type of weather on the card they determine what kind of clothing the doll should wear. They then dress each paper doll, and place it with the correct weather cards.

Clean Up
Store the dolls in storage envelopes; keep the boy and his clothes in one, and the girl and her clothes in another.

Helpful Hints
You may put out all the weather cards at one time, or you may wish to put out the ones that are appropriate to the weather you are experiencing.

Rainy Day

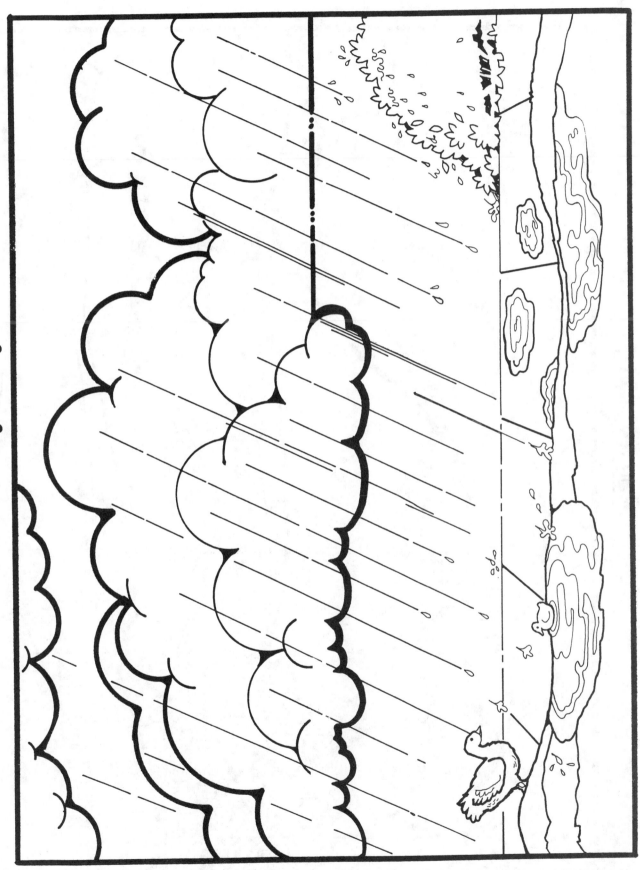

Snowy Day

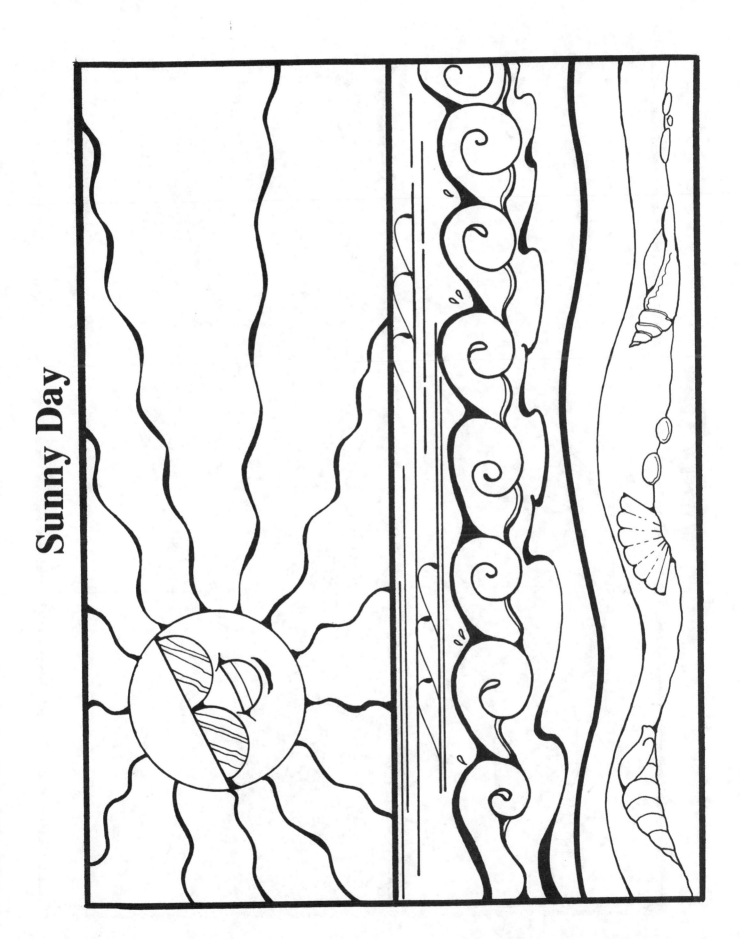

Sunny Day

Windy Day

Paper Dolls

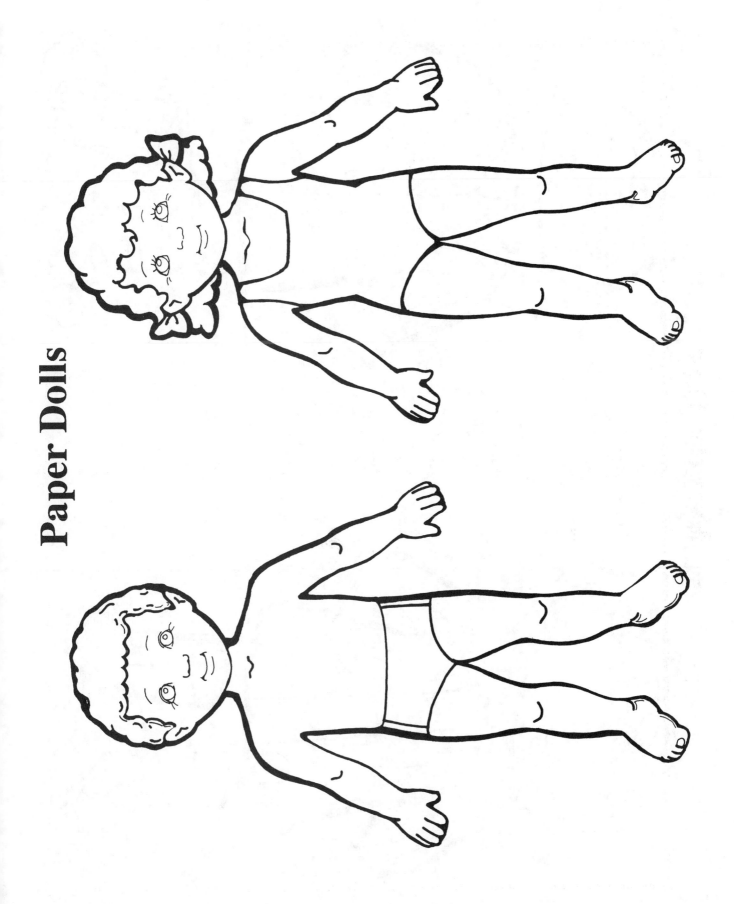

Rainy Day Clothes

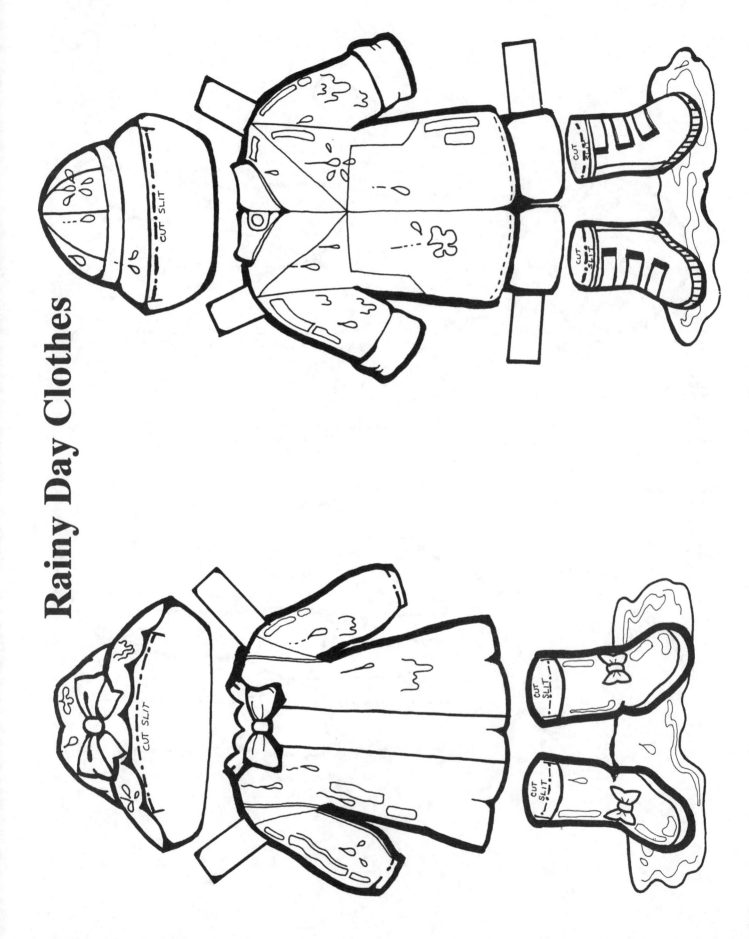

Snowy Day Clothes

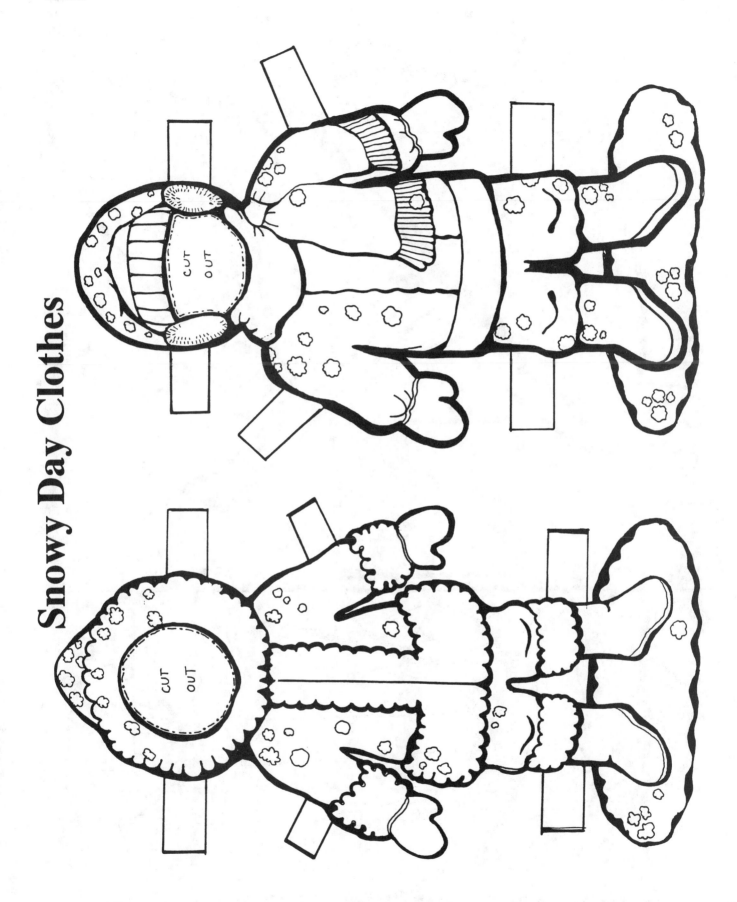

Sunny Day Clothes

Windy Day Clothes

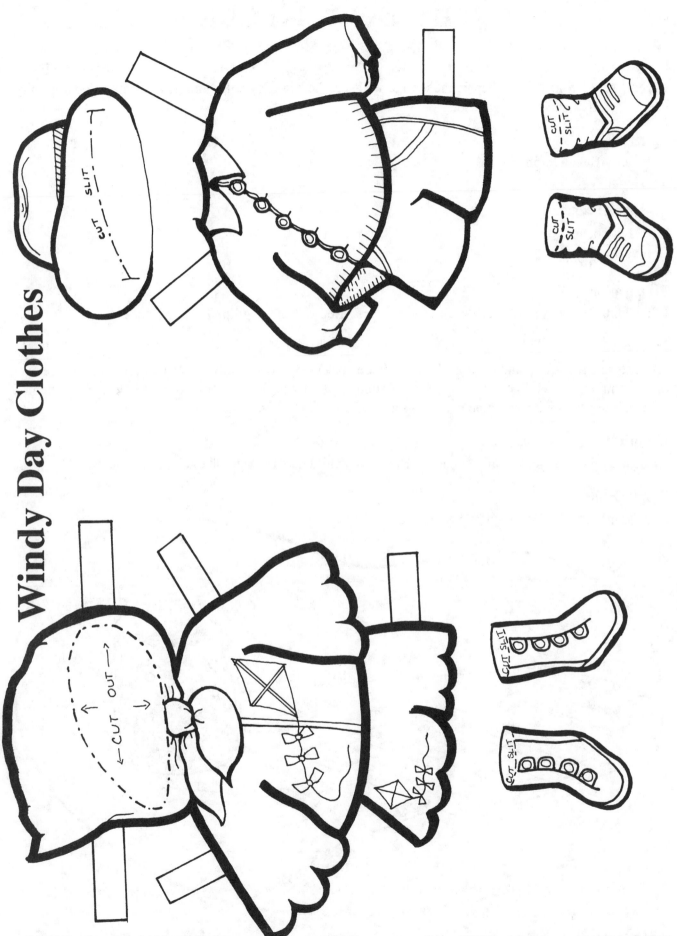

Jelly Bean Graph

Purpose

Given a set of colored jelly beans, the learner will sort the beans by color and learn to make a bar graph using the jelly bean graphing sheet.

Materials

- Jelly Bean Graph (page 243)
- Crayons
- Large container
- Jelly beans
- Tablespoon

Preparation

Fill a container with jelly beans of different colors. Reproduce the graph for each student.

Instructions

Students use the spoon and take out 12-15 jelly beans. They sort the jelly beans by color and lay them on the number of spaces on the graph for the number of jelly beans they have of that color. They then color in the graph with the same color crayon.

Clean-Up

Close the lid on the jelly bean container. Have each child take their graph back to their seats.

Helpful Hints

Jelly beans can also be stored in plastic eggs.

Jelly Bean Graph

	1	2	3	4	5	6	7	8	9	10
Red										
Orange										
Yellow										
Green										
Blue										
Purple										
Pink										
White										
Black										

Wind Sock

Purpose
After studying the weather the learner will create a windsock to determine which way the wind blows.

Materials
- Construction paper
- Streamers
- Crayons
- Staples

- Scissors
- Paper punchers
- String

Preparation
Have paper ready to use. Show children how to roll the paper into a cylinder.

Instructions
Give children a sheet of construction paper and have them decorate it using crayons. Roll it into a cylinder shape and staple. Cut streamers and staple them onto the bottom of the cylinder. Punch two holes at the top of the cylinder. Put string through to hold up the wind sock. Children may create 3-D effects by added pieces that stand out from the cylinder. See the illustrations below.

Clean-Up
Pick up all scraps of paper and recycle. For easy clean-up have students who are punching holes stand over a trash can.

Helpful Hints
Hold onto the wind socks and on a windy day take the class outside to run in the wind with them.

Peter Rabbit

Purpose
The learner retells the story of Peter Rabbit by using the puppets provided.

Materials
- *The Tale of Peter Rabbit*
- Puppet Patterns (page 246)
- Craft Sticks
- Tape
- Scissors
- Crayons
- Stapler

Preparation
Reproduce the patterns for *The Tale of Peter Rabbit*. Read the story *The Tale of Peter Rabbit* by Beatrix Potter (Penguin, 1902; 1987) to the class. Leave the book at the center for children to read again.

Instructions
Children color and cut out the patterns for the puppets. They attach the craft stick to the back of the puppets with tape. They then may retell the story by looking at the copy of the book.

Clean-Up
Pick up scraps and supplies.

Helpful Hints
A little book version of *The Tale of Peter Rabbit* can be found on pages 247-252. You may wish to make a copy or have students make copies for use with their stick puppets.

Peter Rabbit Puppets

Little Book

My Little Book of

The Tale of
Peter Rabbit

The
End

Little Book

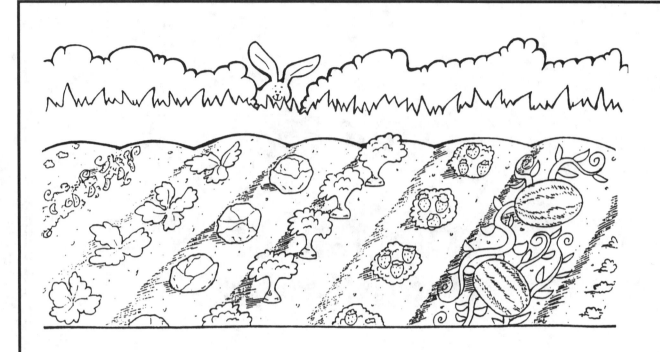

One day Peter Rabbit went in to Mr. McGregor's garden.

1

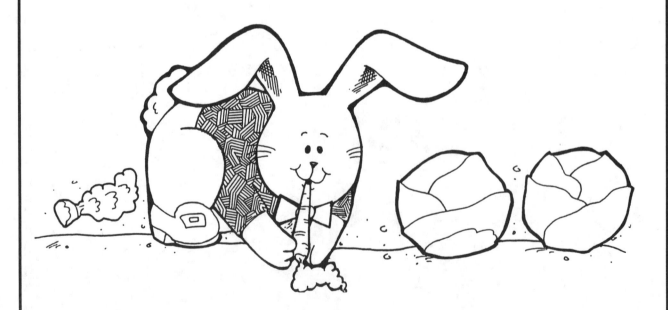

He ate French beans, lettuce, and radishes.
The he saw Mr. McGregor.

2

Little Book

Mr. McGregor ran after him.

3

Mr. McGregor almost caught him, but Peter got out just in time.

4

Little Book

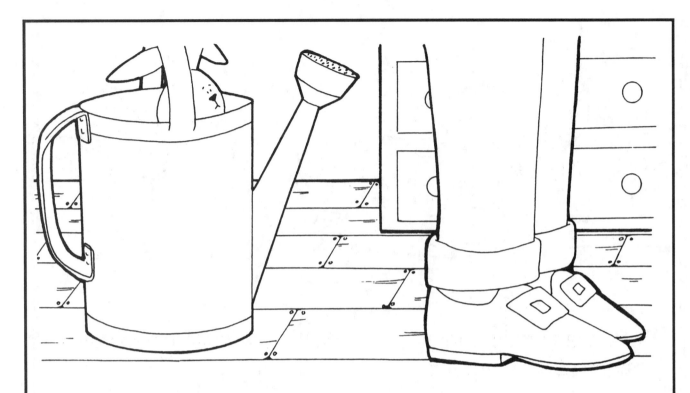

Peter hid in the watering can in the tool-shed.

5

Then Peter sneezed and Mr. McGregor came after him again.

Peter hopped out of the watering can.

6

Little Book

Peter was lost in the garden.   He saw a white cat looking at some fish in a pond.

Then he saw Mr. McGregor hoeing his garden.

7

Just past him Peter saw the gate.

8

Little Book

Peter ran very fast and slipped under the gate.

9

When he got home Peter felt sick.

His mother gave him some tea and put him to bed.

10

St. Patrick's Day

Purpose

The learner will become more familiar with the country of Ireland and St. Patrick's Day.

Materials

- Green, orange, and white crayons
- Pattern (page 254)

Preparation

Reproduce the pattern for children to read and color. Make a sample Irish flag to keep at this center.

Instructions

Share some information with the children about St. Patrick's Day. Have them read the information and then color in the flags.

Clean-Up

Leave the papers stacked neatly when finished with the flag.

Helpful Hints

A real flag and a map of Ireland can be hung up at the center for students to enjoy.

St. Patrick's Day

St. Patrick's Day is celebrated on March 17th. Patrick is the patron saint of Ireland. He helped teach people to read and write. The day St. Patrick died, March 17th, is a national holiday in Ireland.

Here is a picture of the flag of the Republic of Ireland. Color the left section green, the center section white and the right section orange.

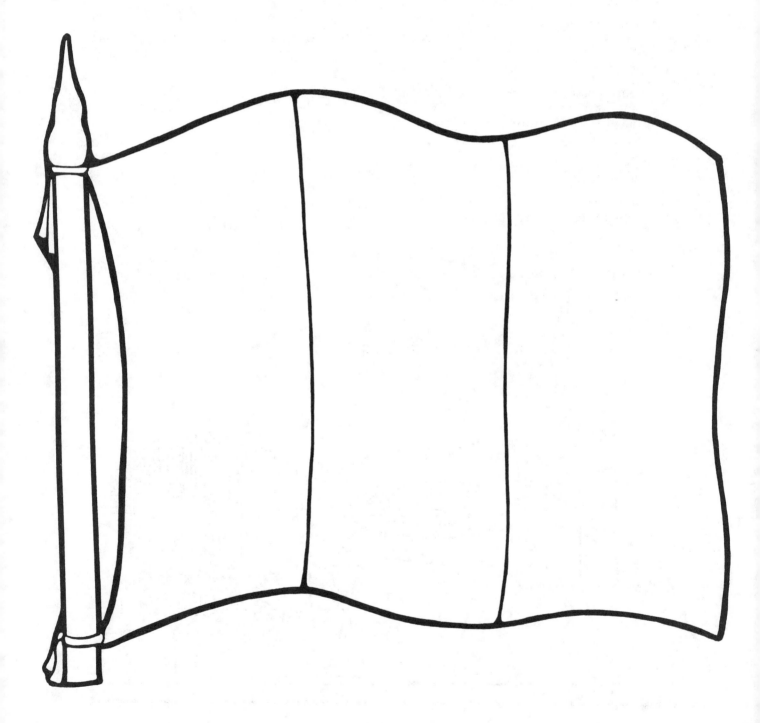

Story Starters

Purpose
Given a story starter, the learner will brainstorm and write a creative story. Children may also illustrate their stories.

Materials
- Story starters (page 256)
- Index cards
- Story paper (pages 381-383)
- Markers
- Pencils
- Crayons
- Can or envelopes

Preparation
Reproduce the story starters. Tape them onto index cards. Put them in a can or an envelope at the center for students to use. Provide story paper.

Instructions
Have students select a story starter. They take a piece of writing paper and copy the story starter onto their paper. Children write an ending to the story starter and illustrate the story. They should be prepared to share the story with the class.

Clean-Up
Put all pencils, markers, and crayons in their appropriate storage containers. Children may take completed stories to their seats.

Helpful Hints
You may wish to write story starters of your own that apply to the material you are currently teaching.

Story Starters *(cont.)*

The following are sentences that could be used as possible story starters.

I was walking along the beach when suddenly . . .

I dialed a number and guess who answered?

Once upon a time, long, long, ago . . .

I can hardly wait until . . .

If I were a giant . . .

If my ruler was a magic wand, I would . . .

The day I went to the moon, I . . .

My dad is funny when . . .

I was really scared when . . .

If I were invisible . . .

Magnets

Purpose
By manipulating magnets, children will learn which things have a magnetic pull.

Materials
- A tray for storage
- Many different sized magnets
- An assortment of objects
- Optional work sheet (page 258)
- A pencil

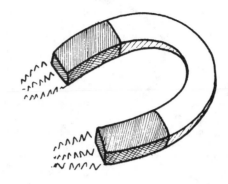

Preparation
Take the tray and put a variety of objects on it. Make sure to include some that will attract a magnet.

Instructions
Using any of the magnets provided, the children will find out which objects on the tray have an attraction to the magnet. Have students use the magnet and try to attract the object. Have them sort the objects into two groups, one for the objects attracted to the magnet, the other for the objects not attracted. If you wish, have children complete the work sheet that goes with the experiment.

Clean-Up
Lay all magnets and objects on the tray. Have children turn their work sheets in for checking.

Helpful Hints
The following objects could be displayed on the tray: key, eraser, cork, bottle top, pair of scissors, rubber band, feather, nail, paper clip, thimble, spoon, screw, penny, nickel, and foil.

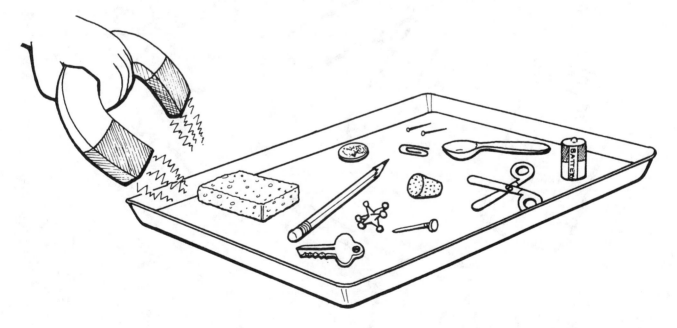

Magnets

Put a circle around those objects a magnet attracts.

Sentence Building

Purpose
The child will arrange word cards to form a complete sentence.

Materials
- Word cards (pages 260-261)
- Scissors
- Index cards
- Box
- Tape or glue

Preparation
To prepare for this center, reproduce the sentences or write a sentence on construction paper. Cut the words in the sentence apart and glue each word onto an index card. Put all word cards for one sentence in an envelope. These envelopes should be numbered and stored in a box.

Instructions
Students select an envelope from the storage box. They take out all the word cards and lay them on the table. They arrange the word cards to form a complete sentence.

Clean-Up
After creating a sentence, place the word cards back into the envelope. Put the envelope in the storage box.

Helpful Hints
You may choose to write your own sentences for the this center. Children enjoy building and reading sentences about themselves and their classmates.

Word Card Sentences

We come to school each day.

At recess we play.

I like math.

It is fun to learn about science.

Word Card Sentences *(cont.)*

I eat lunch with my friends.

It is important to listen.

We need to cooperate.

Let's obey safety rules.

Contraction Trucks

Purpose
Using the trucks and wheels, the learner can match two words that create a contraction.

Materials
- Pattern (page 263)
- Oaktag
- Storage envelope
- Answer key
- Thin marker

Preparation
For every truck reproduced onto oaktag, reproduce two wheels onto oaktag. Use the marker; and on the truck write the contraction, and on the wheels write the two words that form the contraction. Put all the trucks and wheels into the storage envelope. Create an answer key.

Instructions
Children take the envelope and go to the floor. They lay out all the contraction trucks and wheels. Read each contraction on the trucks; match two wheels to the truck, each containing words that form the contraction. For example, if the truck has the contraction "can't" written on it, they find the wheels "can" and "not" to place on the truck. Have students check their work with the answer key.

Clean-Up
Put all trucks and wheels in the envelope. Place the envelope on the center table.

Truck and Wheel Patterns

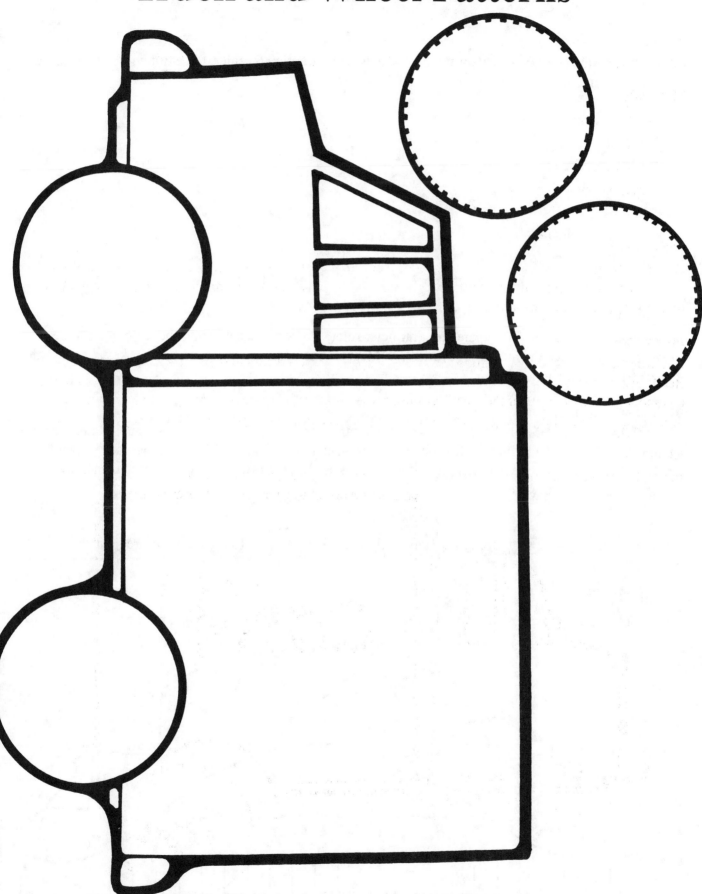

Measuring with Centimeters

Purpose
By measuring the length or width of various objects with a centimeter ruler, the child will become more familiar with this unit of measurement.

Materials
- Centimeter ruler (page 265)
- Tray
- Ten objects
- Pencils
- Measurement chart
- Recording sheet (page 266)
- A prepared answer key in an envelope

Preparation
Provide centimeter rulers or prepare the centimeter ruler. Prepare a sheet listing the ten objects to be measured. Reproduce the measuring worksheet. Measure the items and create an answer key. Leave it at the center in an envelope.

Instructions
Have children take a prepared sheet and write their names at the top. They are to measure all items on the tray. They are then to find the first object that is written on the sheet. They can measure its length or width (depending on the instructions on the sheet) with the centimeter ruler and record the answer on the sheet. They can use the answer key to check their work.

Clean-Up
Place all objects on the tray. Return the answer key to the envelope. Take your measurement sheet to your seat.

Helpful Hints
The following objects can be used at this center: pencil, milk carton, eraser, book, marker.

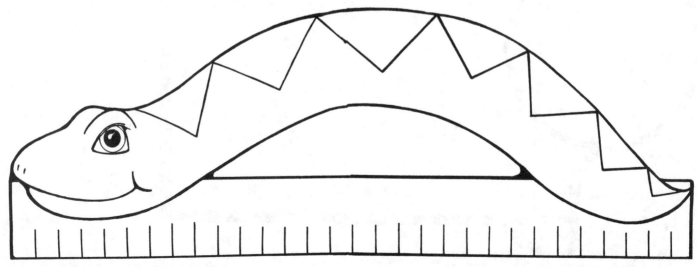

Centimeter Ruler

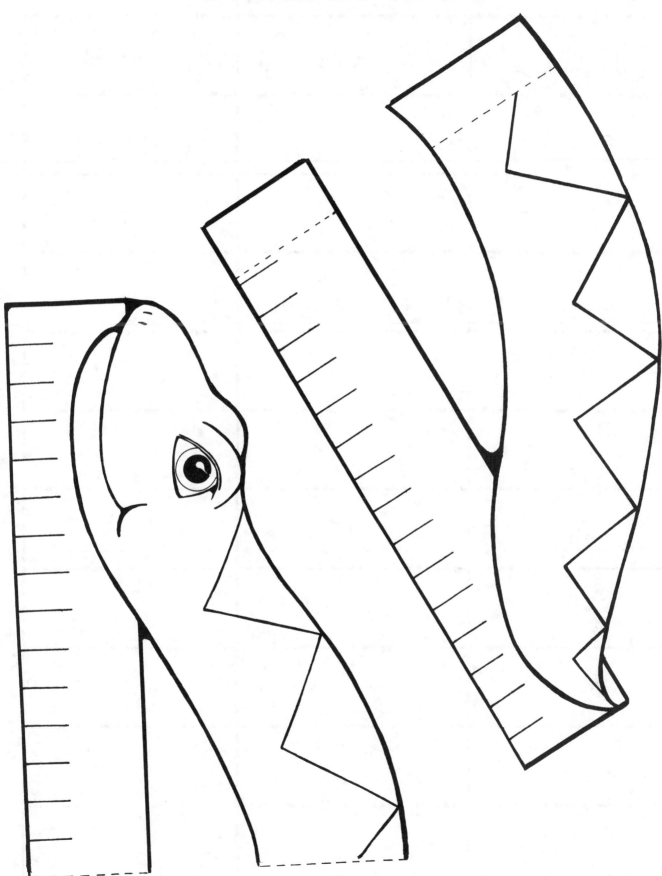

April

Measurement Chart

Items to Measure	Height	Width

Plants and Parts

Purpose
Using a set of pictures, children will determine which part of each plant they eat: stem, root, leaves, flower.

Materials
- Chart (page 268)
- Cards (pages 269-270)
- Storage Envelopes
- Crayons

Preparation
Reproduce the chart and the picture cards. Color and laminate. Put the cards into storage envelopes. Prepare an answer key. Leave in an envelope for children to use when they are finished. The answers are:

Fruit: tomato, green beans, zucchini, pepper

Roots: carrots

Seeds: corn, peas

Tuber: potato, onion

Leaves: cabbage, lettuce

Flower: broccoli

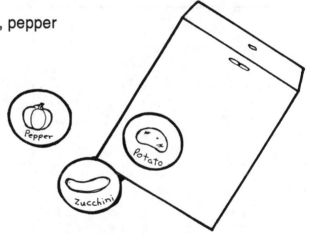

Instructions
Have children look at the pictures of the foods that we eat that are plants. Have them decide what part of the plant we eat and lay it onto the chart under the correct heading.

Clean Up
Put the cards back into the storage envelopes.

Helpful Hints
Bring in some real fruits and vegetables for the children to see. Leave them at the center.

What Part of the Plant Do We Eat?

Fruit

Root

Flower

Seeds

Tuber

Leaves

Plant and Parts Cards

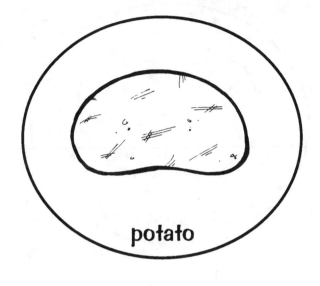

potato

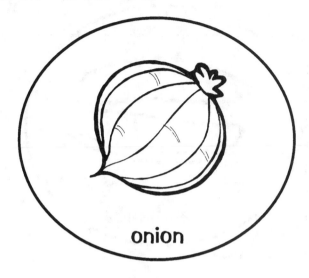

onion

broccoli

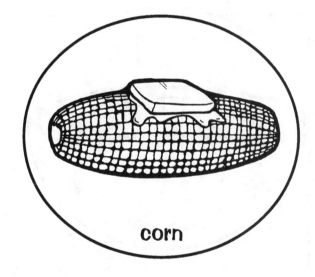

corn

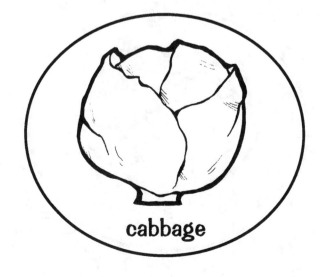

cabbage

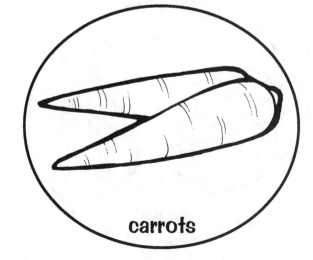

carrots

Plant and Parts Cards *(cont.)*

green beans

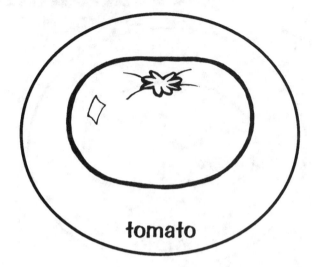

tomato

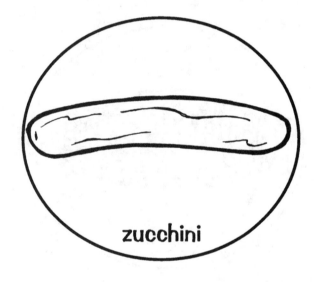

zucchini

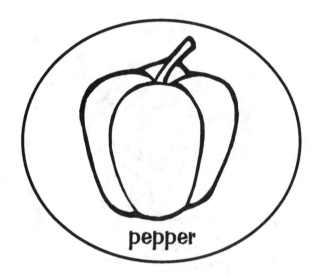

pepper

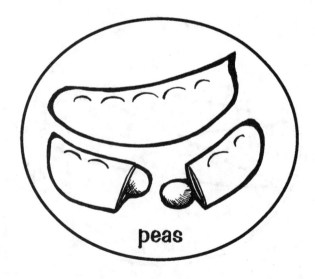

peas

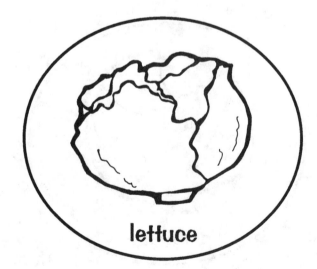

lettuce

Planting

Purpose
Children will determine if seeds can grow in something other than soil by planting seeds in cotton and on a piece of sponge.

Materials

- Egg shells in carton
- Cotton balls
- Mustard seeds
- Water pitcher

- Large area
- Small pieces of sponge
- Tart tins
- Grass seed

Preparation
Gather egg shells and egg cartons. Make sure egg shells are dry.

Instructions
Students should:

1) Label one section of the egg carton with their names. Place a cotton ball in the egg shell. Place 2-3 mustard seeds on the cotton ball. Students should write their names on the bottom of the egg carton.

2) Take a small piece of sponge; place it in a tart tin. Pour water over the sponge. Drop several seeds onto the sponge.

Clean-Up
Throw away any extra egg shells. Store seeds separately.

Helpful Hints
Children might keep a daily journal of what happens; they could also make predictions and record what they think will happen. A recording sheet is provided on page 272.

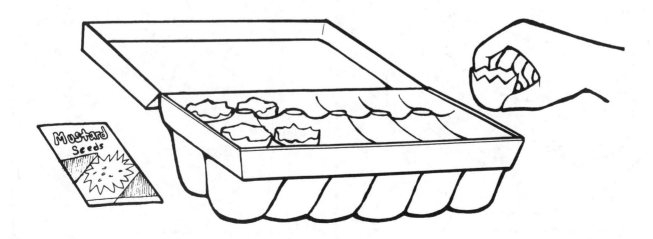

Recording Sheet

Fill in the sentences and draw pictures for each day your teacher tells you.

Day _____

Day _____

Day _____

Day _____

Toothpick Shapes

Purpose

The learner will paste toothpicks on construction paper in order to make and reorganize simple geometric shapes.

Materials

- Toothpicks
- Resealable bags
- Construction paper
- Glue
- A lid

Preparation

Have construction paper ready for children to glue the toothpicks onto.

Instructions

Children first squeeze some glue into the lid. They select a piece of colored construction paper. They dip the ends of the toothpicks into the glue and make drawings or geometric shapes on the construction paper using the toothpicks. Have them be prepared to share what shapes are in their design.

Clean-Up

Close the glue and seal the bag of toothpicks. Have students take their designs home.

Helpful Hints

To make this center more complicated, the teacher may want to specify the number of toothpicks to be used in a design. For example: Use 12 toothpicks and make a design with three triangles. Another option is to use the sheet provided on page 274 and have children fill in or copy the designs with toothpicks.

Toothpick Design

Hot-Air Balloon

"Baa, Baa, Black Sheep"

Purpose

Children will retell the story of "Baa, Baa, Black Sheep" using flannel pieces.

Materials

- Flannel Board
- Flannel Board Patterns (page 277)
- Scissors
- Storage Envelope
- Poem (page 276)

Preparation

Use the patterns to make flannel pieces for the poem. Recite the words with the children and leave a copy at the center for the children to use as they use the flannel board pieces to act out the story.

Instructions

Have children read the poem "Baa, Baa, Black Sheep." They should move the flannel pieces around as they read or recite the rhyme.

Clean-Up

Place all flannel pieces into the storage envelope.

Helpful Hints

A magnetic board may be substituted for a flannel board. Pieces can then be cut out of heavy paper and magnetic strips can be placed onto the back of each piece.

"Baa, Baa, Black Sheep"

Baa, Baa, Black Sheep

Have you any wool?

Yes, sir, yes, sir,

Three bags full;

One for the master,

And one for the dame,

And one for the little boy

Who lives down the lane.

Baa, Baa, Black Sheep

Have you any wool?

Yes, sir, yes, sir,

Three bags full.

"Baa, Baa, Black Sheep" Patterns

Where Do I Grow?

Purpose

Children will be able to identify where some crops are grown.

Materials

- Map (page 280)
- Story (page 279)
- Scissors
- Glue
- Crayons

Preparation

Reproduce the story and the map. Read the story with the children.

Instructions

Children will find out in which states the crops in the story are grown. They will color, cut them out, and paste them onto the map.

Clean-Up

Pick up any scraps that have been left about. Leave the center neat for the next user.

Helpful Hints

Use the map of the United States. Help children find their home state and something that is grown there.

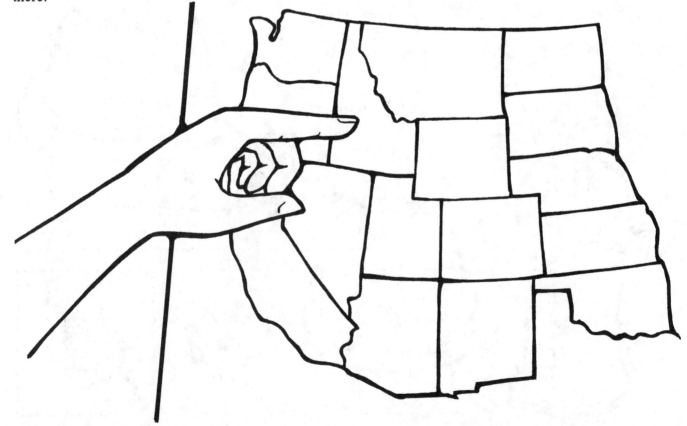

Where Do I Grow? *(cont.)*

Food grows on farms in many states. Corn grows in Iowa. Potatoes grow in Idaho. Oranges grow in Florida. In Montana they grow wheat. What food grows in your state?

Cut out the crops and glue them to the states in which they grow.

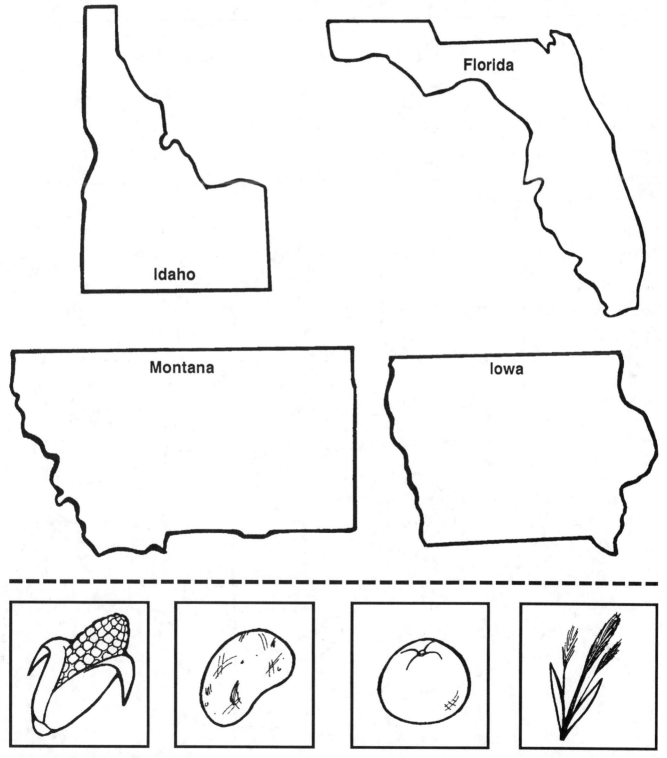

United States Map

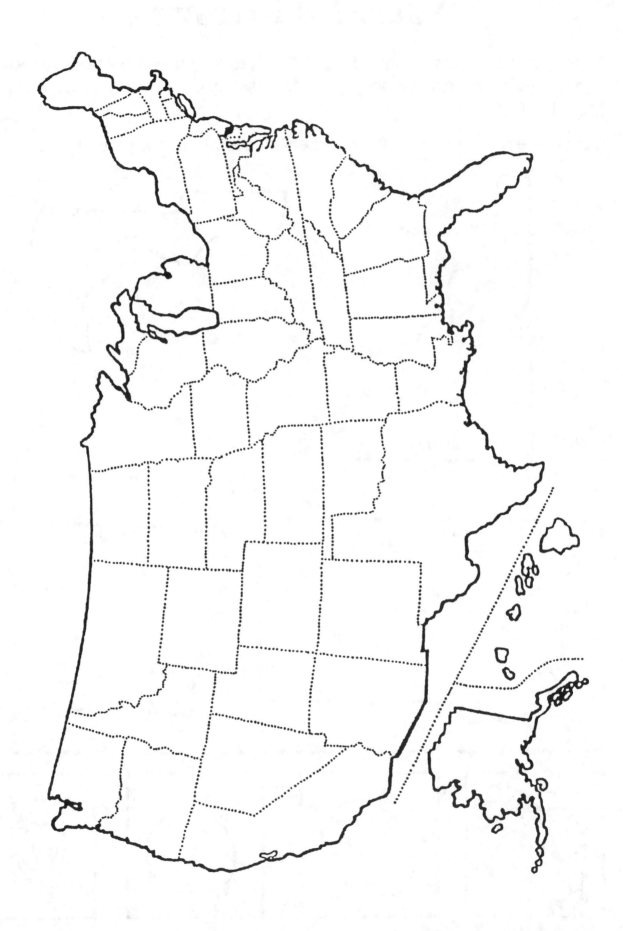

I Planted a Seed

Purpose

Children will write a fantasy story about planting a magical seed.

Materials

- Story paper
- Pencils
- Story of "Jack and the Beanstalk" (pages 282-283)

Preparation

Reproduce the story of "Jack and the Beanstalk." Read this or any version of this classic story to the class before they begin working at this center.

Instructions

Children will read the story "Jack and the Beanstalk." After they do, have them write a story of their own about planting magic beans.

Clean-Up

Make sure there are copies of the stories or the book out for children to read at the center.

Helpful Hints

John Howe has a beautifully illustrated version of this story. Paul Galdone has also created a rhyming version. See bibliography on page 384.

"Jack and the Beanstalk"

Once upon a time there was a poor widow who lived in a cottage with her son Jack. Jack was a very good boy, but liked to daydream about adventures instead of doing chores. One year after a very dry summer, the widow and Jack had little left to eat. Even the grass that fed their cow Milky White had died, which meant the cow would have to be sold. So Jack set off to the market, telling his mother he would get a good price for Milky White.

On his way to town, Jack saw an old man with a strange hat sitting beside the road. The old man said, "What a beautiful cow! I have no money, but I will trade these five magic beans for her," he said as he held out his hand. Being more adventurous than practical, Jack made the trade and went happily home.

When he got home his mother was furious with the trade and threw the magic beans out the window. The next morning Jack awoke to see something extraordinary outside his bedroom window. A beanstalk had grown overnight and reached way into the sky.

Jack ran outside and climbed the magic beanstalk into the clouds. When he got above the clouds he saw a castle. A woman with a milkpail said that the castle belonged to her husband who was a very mean giant. Jack asked her for some milk and the wife said yes. However she cautioned Jack about the giant's bad temper and his fondness for little boys on toast for breakfast.

Suddenly they heard a big voice. "Fe Fi Fo Fum, I smell the blood of an Englishman. Be he alive or be he dead, I'll grind his bones to make my bread!" The giant had returned. The wife quickly hid Jack in the oven while she fed her husband two cows for breakfast. The giant then took out three bags of gold and fell asleep while counting the pieces. Jack popped out of the oven, took one bag, and then ran to the magic beanstalk. When he returned home, he showed his mother the gold. She was quite pleased.

"Jack..." *(cont.)*

After some time, the gold had been spent, and Jack went up the beanstalk again. This time the giant's wife did not trust him but wanted to find out what had happened to the gold. So, she fed him again. But they were soon interrupted by a thundering voice. "Fe Fi Fo Fum, I smell the blood of an Englishman. Be he alive or be he dead, I'll grind his bones to make my bread!" Into the oven again went Jack. After eating three sheep for lunch, the giant called for his magic hen who began to lay golden eggs. Soon he fell asleep and Jack popped out of the oven, grabbed the hen, and scurried home. His mother was delighted with the hen.

A few months later, Jack yearned for adventure and climbed the beanstalk again. This time, the giant and wife were nowhere in sight. He decided to hide in the woodbox and wait for the giant to bring out more gold or magic hens.

"Fe Fi Fo Fum, I smell the blood of an Englishman. Be he alive or be he dead, I'll grind his bones to make my bread!" This time the giant's wife smelled the boy too. They looked in the oven and everywhere else, but couldn't find him.

Then the giant brought out a magic harp that played such beautiful music that they both fell asleep. Jack popped out of the woodbox, stole the harp, and sped home.

But the harp cried out, "Master, help me," and woke the giant. He chased Jack down the beanstalk. Jack yelled down to his mother to bring him the ax. Once on the ground, Jack got the ax, chopped the beanstalk, and the giant crashed to the earth and broke his neck.

Jack and his mother lived happily ever after with the magic hen and the golden harp and the mean giant never had little boys on toast for breakfast again.

Liquid Measurement

Purpose

By filling the containers and pouring water from one container into another, the child will learn to associate an amount and size with the words cups, pint, quart, and gallon. Children will also begin to experiment with how many of one container will fill another.

Materials

- Containers: cup, pint, quart, gallon
- Liquid Measurement Chart (page 285)
- Pitcher
- Water
- Paper towels

Preparation

Prepare the Liquid Measurement Chart. Laminate to waterproof it.

Instructions

Children should first take the pitcher to the sink and fill it with water, then fill and experiment with the containers provided.

Clean-Up

Empty all the containers at the sink. Use paper towels to dry off the containers. Also, wipe up any excess water that may have spilled at the center table. Recycle the towels and sit all containers on the center table. Children should try to remember answers to each question. They may be asked to demonstrate and share answers.

Helpful Hints

This learning center should be positioned close to the sink.

The teacher could use household items that are the appropriate size for the containers. It works best to provide plastic containers that are clear, so the learner can see if the container is full. If the containers being used at this center are not already marked, label each with the appropriate word: cup, pint, quart, gallon.

Liquid Measurement Chart

Look at the chart, try to answer each of the questions.

1. Find the cup. Use it to fill the pint. How many cups in a pint?

2. Find the pint. Use it to fill the quart. How many pints in a quart?

3. Find the quart. Use it to fill the gallon. How many quarts in a gallon?

4. Find the cup. Use it to fill the quart. How many cups in a quart?

5. Find the pint. Use it to fill the gallon. How many pints in a gallon?

6. Find the cup. Use it to fill the gallon. How many cups in a gallon?

Punctuation Clips

Purpose

The learner will read a set of sentences written on strips and attach the appropriate punctuation mark to each.

Materials

- Sentence strips (pages 287-288)
- 10 clothespins
- Thin-tipped marker
- Storage container for the clothes pins

Preparation

Reproduce the sentence strips by either photocopying onto index paper or writing them onto sentence strip paper. On the back of the strip write the proper punctuation mark. On the clothespins write the punctuation marks required to finish the sentences.

Instructions

Children will lay all sentence strips on the floor. They will read each strip quietly and decide if the sentence is a telling sentence, an asking sentence, or an exciting sentence. If it is a telling sentence, clip a clothespin with a period on it to the sentence strip. If it is an asking sentence, clip a clothespin with a question mark on it to the sentence. If it is a sentence showing excitement, clip a clothespin with an exclamation mark on it to the strip. After attaching a clothespin to each sentence, have students turn each strip over to check work.

Clean-Up

Remove all the clothespins from the sentence strips and put clothespins in the container provided. Lay all strips in a neat pile on the center table.

Sentence Strips

The little girl likes to jump rope	He ate an apple for lunch	They like to ride their bikes	The birthday party was fun	Please put on your coat

Sentence Strips

What is the puppy's name	How old are you	Who gave you that piece of candy	Where do you live	Did you like the movie

Paper Cup Stack-Ups

Purpose

By stacking cups, children can review such skills as recognizing the letters of the alphabet, and ordinal words, and counting by twos.

Materials

- Styrofoam cups
- Storage bags

Preparation

Stack styrofoam cups. Then turn them over. The teacher may wish to create three sets of cups creating three styrofoam stack-up activities. Label the sets of cups with the letters of the alphabet, ordinal words, and numbers to count by twos. Write labels on the outside rim close to the bottom. Store each stack-up activity in a separate bag.

Instructions

Students select a bag containing a stack-up activity. Lay out all of the styrofoam cups. Stack the cups by placing one on top of another to progress through the alphabet, ordinal words, or counting by twos. Complete one set of styrofoam stacks and put them away before getting out another set. Do all three styrofoam stack-up activities.

Clean-Up

Make sure all styrofoam cups are in the appropriate activity bag. Set all bags on the center table.

Helpful Hints

Styrofoam stack-up activities can also be developed for rhyming words, alphabetical order, number words, order counting by fives and tens. Two or more sets of cups containing rhyming words may be mixed together and then stacked with those that rhyme. For example, one set of cups can have cat, rat, sat, and bat on them and another set can have hit, pit, sit, bit. All cups are placed in a bag; the child sets them on the table and stacks them into two towers of rhyming words. This can be made self-checking if the cups are numbered on the inside. Children look to see if the numbers are in the correct order.

Pattern Block Shapes

Purpose

By manipulating shapes, the child will become familiar with the characteristics of each shape. The child will also associate a name with each shape. Children will create designs and patterns through the manipulation of shapes.

Materials

- Black construction paper
- Glue
- Pencils
- Resealable bags
- Shape patterns (pages 291-294)
- Index paper

Preparation

Reproduce the shape patterns onto index paper. Cut the shapes out. Place them into resealable bags.

Instructions

Students pick whatever shapes they want to use from the bags. They place the paper shapes on the black paper, positioning into designs. Then students glue the pieces into place.

Clean-Up

After completing a design, put any extra shapes back into the appropriate bag, seal the bags and close the glue. Have children take design back to their seats.

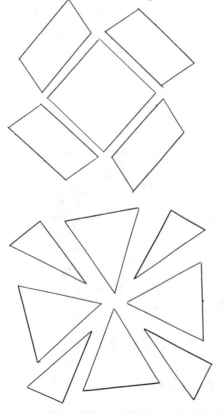
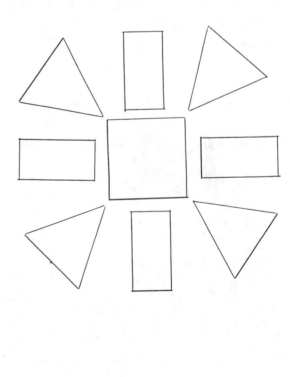

Triangle Pattern Blocks

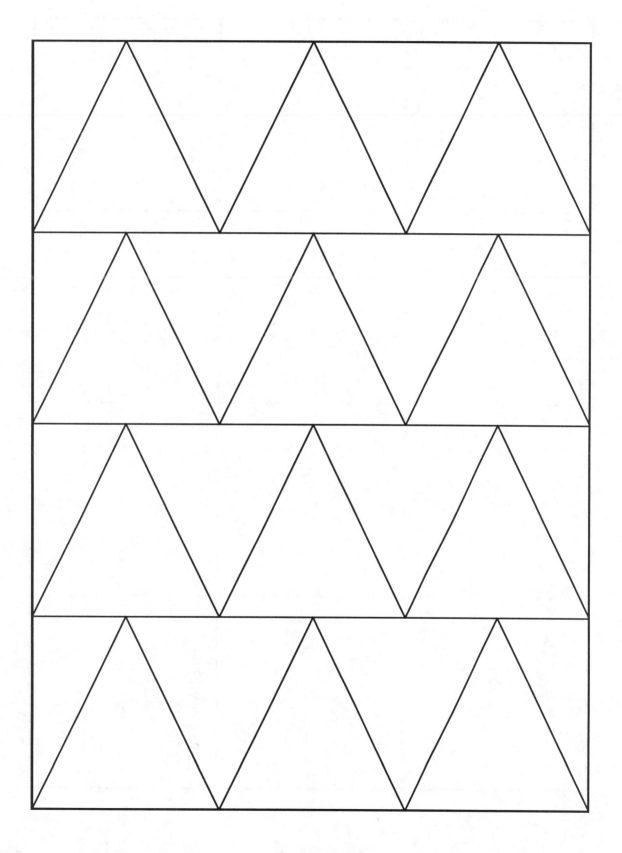

Square Pattern Shapes

Rectangle Pattern Shapes

Parallelogram Pattern Shapes

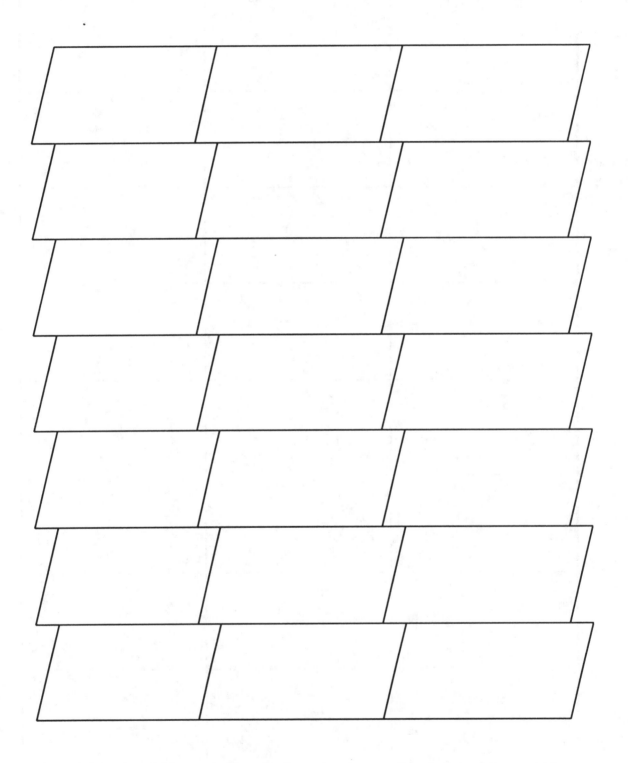

Animals

Purpose
Given a set of animal cards the learner can sort the animals into the following groups: birds, reptiles, fish, amphibians, and mammals.

Materials
- Animal cards (pages 297-301)
- A storage envelope
- Chart (page 296)

Preparation
Reproduce the cards. Color and laminate. Cut cards and put them into labeled envelopes: bird, reptile, fish, amphibian, and mammal. Reproduce and laminate the chart for students to use.

Instructions
Take the storage envelope, remove all of the animal cards. Sort them onto the chart according to their characteristics into the following groups: birds, reptiles, fish, amphibians, and mammals.

Clean Up
Place all animal cards into the storage envelope.

Animal Sorting

Birds

Reptiles

Fish

Amphibians

Mammals

Birds

Amphibians

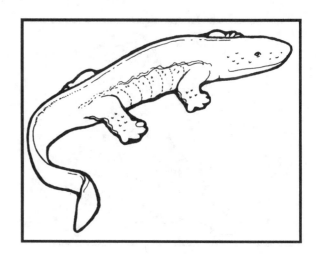

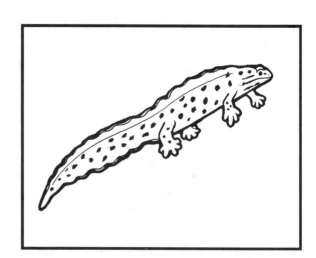

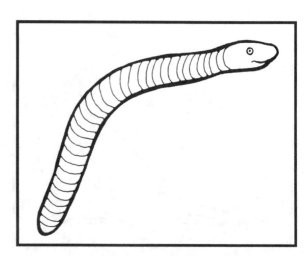

Fish

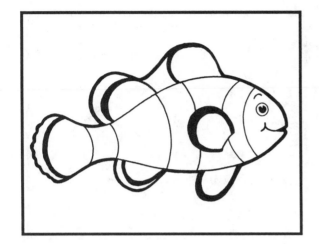

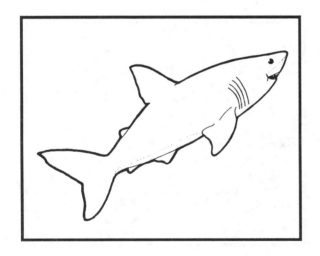

Reptiles

Mammals

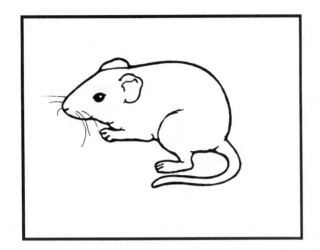 

301

Paper Bag Animal Puppet

Purpose

Children will create a realistic or imaginative animal paper bag puppet.

Materials

- Construction paper
- Lunch bags
- Puppet pieces (pages 303-304)
- Scissors
- Glue
- Crayons
- Markers

Preparation

Have all materials ready for the children. Reproduce the puppet so children can use them to make their puppets.

Instructions

Have students think about a favorite animal. Using construction paper, puppet pieces, and other supplies, they are to create a bag puppet of a favorite animal.

Clean-Up

Cover all glue, recycle scraps, and put back materials.

Puppet Pieces

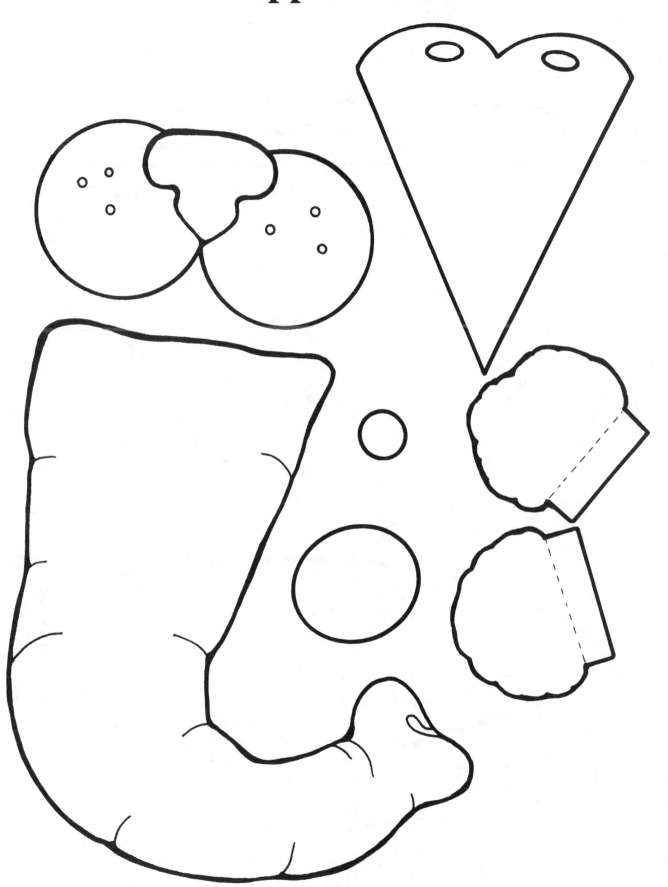

Puppet Pieces *(cont.)*

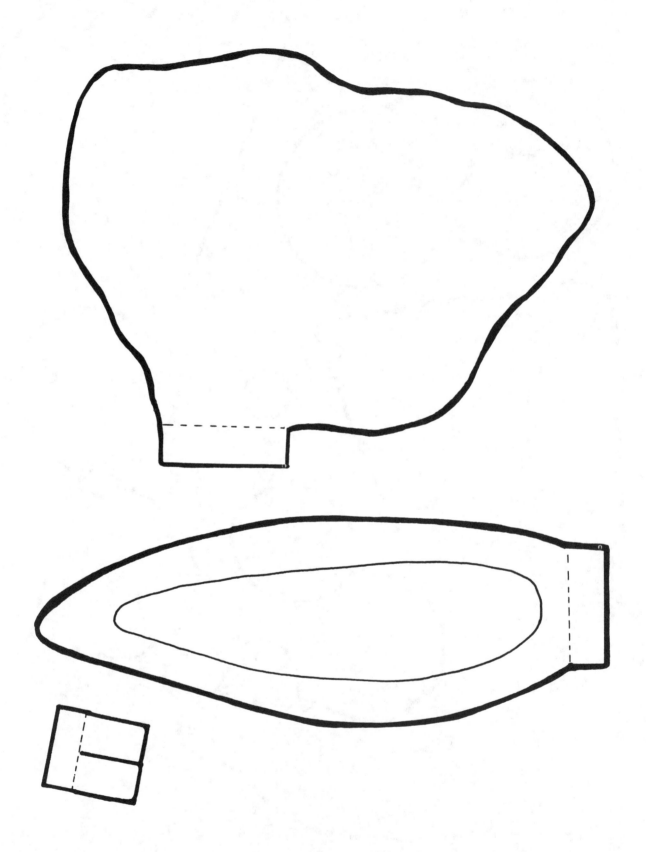

Finger Print Animals

Purpose
By pressing fingers onto an ink pad and then onto paper, children will create finger print animals.

Materials
- Ink pads
- Paper
- Crayons
- Fingerprint Habitats (pages 306-309)

Preparation
Have ink pads ready for children to use. Locate this center near a sink if possible.

Instructions
Children press fingers into the ink pad. They then press their fingers onto paper. Have them use crayons to add legs or other parts to create a finger print animal.

Clean-Up
Make sure the children clean their hands, and that all ink pads are closed.

Helpful Hints
Let children put their animals into a habitat of their choice. They may make the animals on the sheet or complete them on another paper, cut them out and glue them on.

Finger Print Farm

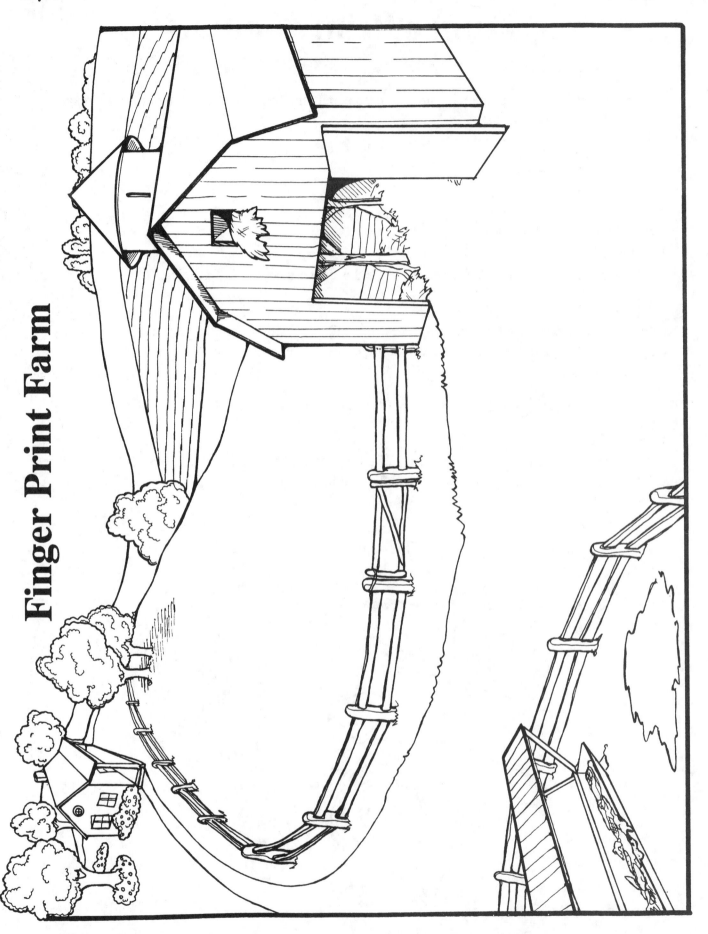

Finger Print Circus

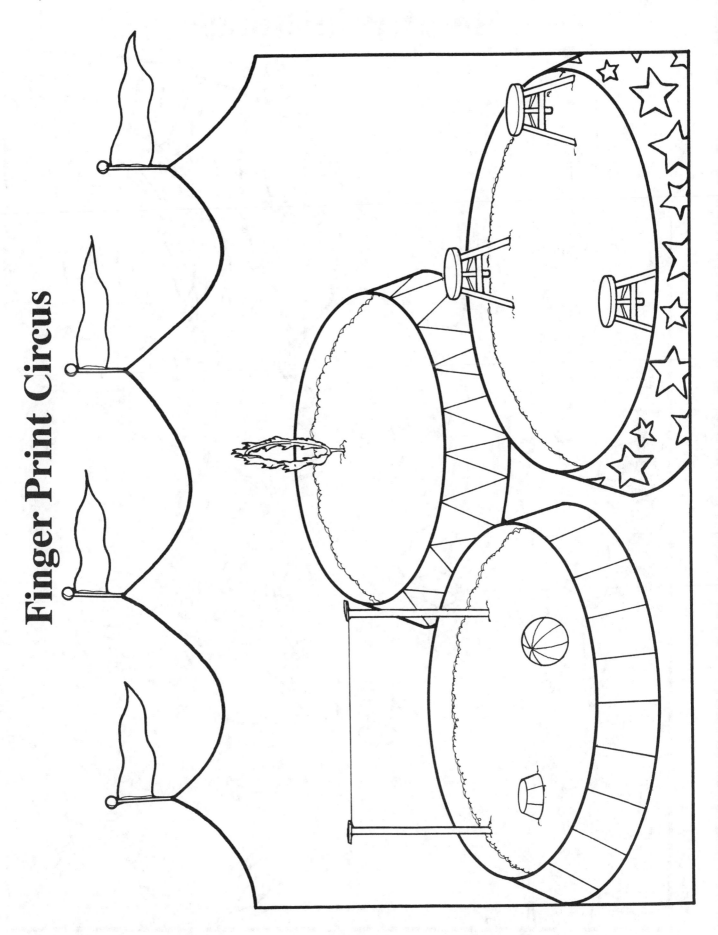

Finger Print Jungle

308

Finger Print Home

"Old MacDonald"

Purpose

Children will tell the story of the farmer, Old MacDonald, using finger puppets and the words to the song.

Materials

- Puppet patterns (pages 312-314)
- "Old MacDonald" (page 311)
- Crayons
- Scissors
- Tape

Preparation

Reproduce the patterns for use at the centers. Before children use the center, sing the song "Old MacDonald."

Instructions

Students will make the finger puppets provided at this center. They color them, cut them out, and use tape to adjust the size to their fingers. Then they may softly sing or retell the story of "Old MacDonald" while using the puppets.

Clean-Up

Put all supplies back where they belong.

Helpful Hints

Although the words are given for a cow, a pig, a duck, and a horse, other animals can be substituted. You may record the whole class singing the song and leave it at the center with a tape recorder for children to listen to. Post the words at the center.

"Old MacDonald"

Old MacDonald had a farm.
E-I-E-I-O;
And on his farm he had a cow,
E-I-E-I-O;

With a moo-moo here and a moo-moo there,
here a moo, there a moo,
everywhere a moo-moo,
Old MacDonald had a farm.
E-I-E-I-O.

Old MacDonald had a farm.
E-I-E-I-O;
And on his farm he had a pig,
E-I-E-I-O;

With an oink-oink here,
and an oink-oink there,
here an oink, there an oink,
everywhere an oink-oink,
Old MacDonald had a farm.
E-I-E-I-O.

Old MacDonald had a farm.
E-I-E-I-O;
And on his farm he had a duck,
E-I-E-I-O;

With a quack-quack here and a quack-quack there,
here a quack, there a quack,
everywhere a quack-quack,
Old MacDonald had a farm.
E-I-E-I-O.

Old MacDonald had a farm.
E-I-E-I-O;
And on his farm he had a horse,
E-I-E-I-O;

With a neigh-neigh here and a neigh-neigh there,
here a neigh, there a neigh,
everywhere a neigh-neigh,
Old MacDonald had a farm.
E-I-E-I-O.

Old McDonald's Farm Animals

Old MacDonald's Farm Animals *(cont.)*

Old MacDonald's Farm Animals (cont.)

Bike Safety

Purpose
Students will become aware of good safety habits when riding a bicycle.

Materials
- Poster (page 317-318)
- Student poster (page 316)
- Bike helmet
- Crayons

Preparation
Reproduce the small chart for each child. Put together the large chart. Color and hang it at the center.

Instructions
Let children practice trying on the bike helmet. Have them read the safety rules and then color in the chart.

Clean-Up
Leave materials for the next student ready to use.

Bike Safety Poster for Children

Bike Safety Rules

1. Walk your bike across the street.
2. Don't ride double on your bike.
3. Wear a bike helmet.
4. Ride bike with traffic.
5. Use bike lanes if possible.
6. Keep your eyes on traffic.
7. Ride at a safe speed.
8. Try to wear bright clothes.

Bike Safety Teacher Poster

1. Walk your bike across the street.

2. Don't ride double on your bike.

3. Wear a bike helmet.

4. Ride bike with traffic.

5. Use bike lanes if possible.

6. Keep your eyes on traffic.

7. Ride at a safe speed.

8. Try to wear bright clothes.

What If...? Stories

Purpose

Children will write a creative story responding to the question, What If...?

Materials

- A card file box
- Index cards
- Writing paper
- Pencils
- Crayons
- Markers
- Story Ideas (pages 320-321)

Preparation

Reproduce the story ideas. Cut the ideas up and attach or copy one onto an index card. Put the index cards into the file box. The last one is incomplete for you to fill in if you wish.

Instructions

Students select a card from the file box and read the idea written on the card. They take a piece of writing paper and develop a story from the idea. Have them illustrate the story and be prepared to share it.

Clean-Up

Place the idea card in the file box. Put all materials away and have student take stories to their seats.

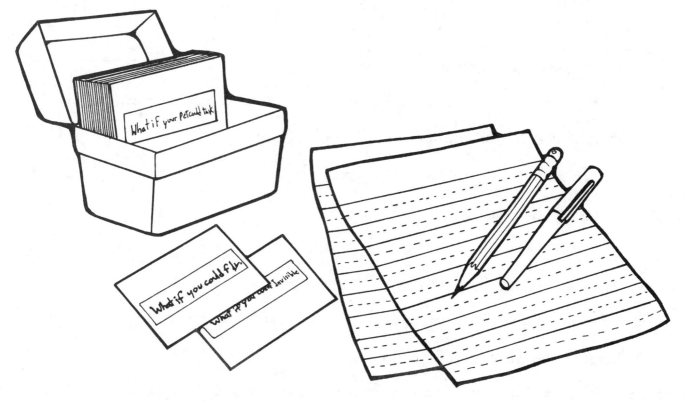

What If...? Story Ideas

1. What if a plane landed in the school yard one day?

2. What if you saw a zebra grazing in front of your house one morning?

3. What if you found a turtle in your bathtub?

4. What if you were traveling in a wagon hundreds of years ago?

5. What if your pet could talk?

6. What if someone gave you three wishes; what would you wish for?

7. What if you were principal for a day; what would you do?

8. What if you were invisible?

9. What if aliens took you for a ride in their spaceship?

10. What if you could fly?

11. What if children did not have to go to school?

12. What if you went on a field trip to the moon?

What If...? Story Ideas (cont.)

13. What if you were a king or a queen in a castle?

14. What if you were an inventor; what would you invent?

15. What if you suddenly shrunk in size; what would you do?

16. What if you could read people's minds?

17. What if there were no telephones?

18. What if it rained for 100 days?

19. What if you could only read one book forever?

20. What if all the water dried up?

21. What if trash was not ever collected?

22. What if all the batteries died?

23. What if the grass were red instead of green?

24. What if

Jungle Animal Sort

Purpose

Given a set of jungle cards the learner will sort the animals according to where they are found: on the land, in the trees, in the water.

Materials

- Animal chart (page 323)
- Animal cards (pages 324-326)
- Storage envelope
- Crayons
- Scissors

Preparation

Reproduce the animals. Color and cut out. Reproduce and place them into a storage envelope. Put the chart together.

Instructions

Children take the envelope with the animals in it. They put the correct animal into the area of the jungle where they are found, land, trees, water.

Clean-Up

Place all cards into the storage envelopes.

Jungle Animal Sort Chart

Put the animals where they belong, on the land, in the trees, or in the water.

Chart (cont.)

324

Jungle Animal Cards

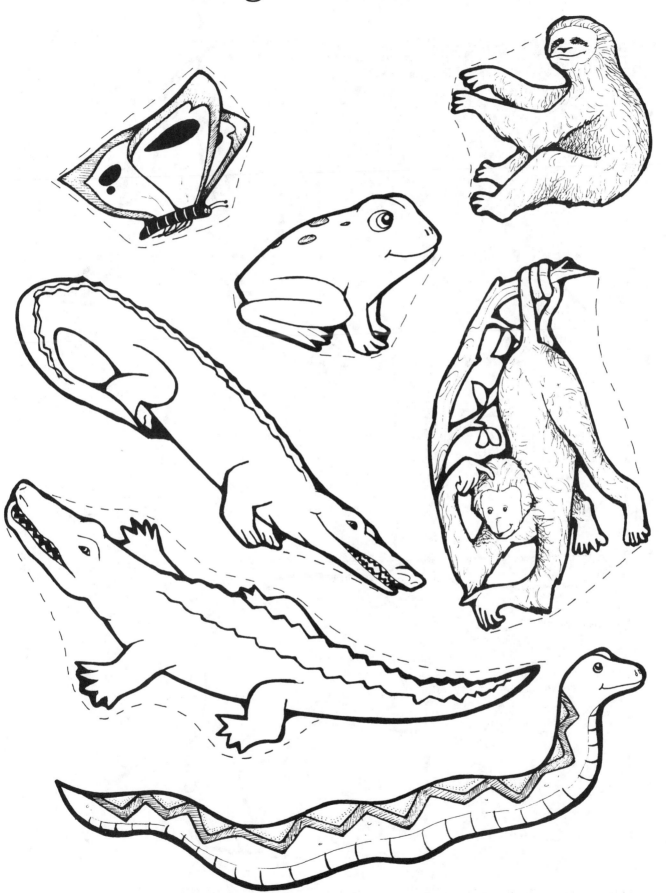

Jungle Animal Cards

Reading Pockets

Purpose

The learner will put word cards in ABC order, arrange word cards to make sentences, and put ordinal words in the correct order on a pocket board.

Materials

- Poster board
- Library book pockets
- Index cards
- Markers
- Word/Sentence cards (pages 328-330)

Preparation

To make this center, attach library book pockets to a poster board. Use index cards to create packets with instructions and activity cards. Use the word cards to create three sets of cards: one for ABC order, one to make sentences, and one for ordinal words. Cut these and glue to index cards. You may make word cards of your own.

Instructions

Have students select a packet of index cards and directions. Follow the directions for each packet. Use the board and place the index cards in the pockets. Have a student or the teacher check the work before going on to the next activity packet.

Clean-Up

Place all cards for one activity together with a rubber band.

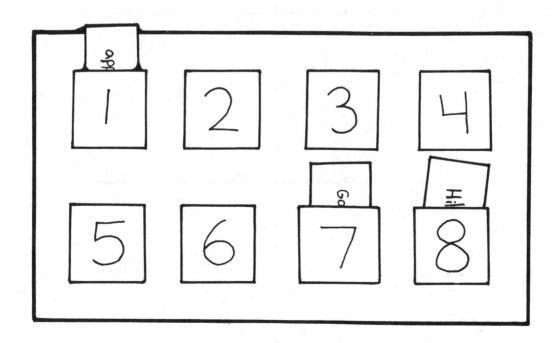

Word Cards for ABC order

apple	happy
bear	teacher
carrot	soup
dog	vegetable
frog	wheel

Sentences for Word Cards

Summer will be here soon.

I will go swimming.

The sun will shine.

Watermelon is a juicy fruit.

Reading in the summer will be fun.

Ordinal Word Cards

First	Second	Third
Fourth	Fifth	Sixth
Seventh	Eighth	Ninth
Tenth	Eleventh	Twelfth

Rubber Band Cards

Purpose
Given a set of pictures on a card, the learner will be able to connect a rubber band to the long or short vowel sound for each.

Materials
- 5-6 rubber band cards
- Rubber bands in a bag
- Heavy white cardboard
- Clip art (pages 333-334)

Preparation
To make rubber band cards, cut heavy white cardboard into 5" x 7" (13 cm x 18 cm) pieces. On the front, draw five pictures down the right side or use the clip art to create your cards. On the left, write vowel sounds. On the side of the card, cut out notches by the pictures and the vowels. On the back, draw dotted lines for self-checking. These dotted lines will be covered when the rubber bands are correctly matching the picture to the appropriate vowel sound.

Instructions
Have students select a rubber band card and five rubber bands. Students look at the pictures on the right side of the card; take one rubber band, slip it around the card; put it in the notch by the picture on the right, and then in the notch on the left by the corresponding vowel sound. Use all five rubber bands and match each picture to its vowel sound. Then turn the card over for self-checking. If the rubber bands cover the dotted lines, the work is correct.

Clean-Up
Take all the rubber bands off the cards. Put the rubber bands in the bag provided. Lay cards on the center table.

Helpful Hints
Rubber band cards can also be created and used for beginning and ending sounds, blends, and math facts.

Rubber Band Card Pattern

Rubber Band Card Clip Art

Rubber Band Card Clip Art *(cont.)*

Short Vowel Rubber Band Card

pup

cat

hill

bed

sock

Long Vowel Rubber Band Card

bee

mice

mule

baby

boat

Commutative Property

Purpose
Children will understand the commutative property in math by selecting an addition fact and then using colorful dot stickers or small stamps to demonstrate each number.

Materials
- Commutative property sheet (page 338)
- Different colored dot stickers or 2 stampers of different colors
- Stamp pad
- Pencil

Preparation
Reproduce the worksheet for each child. Have ready sticky dots or a small stamper.

Instructions
Select a commutative sheet. Pick an addition fact. Write it on one side, then reverse the order of the facts and write it on the other side.

Example: Then use dot stickers or a bingo stamper to illustrate the fact.

2 + 3 = 5

3 + 2 = 5

Clean-Up
Put all dots back onto a sheet of paper that they can be removed from, and put away any stampers and stamp pad.

Commutative Property Sheet

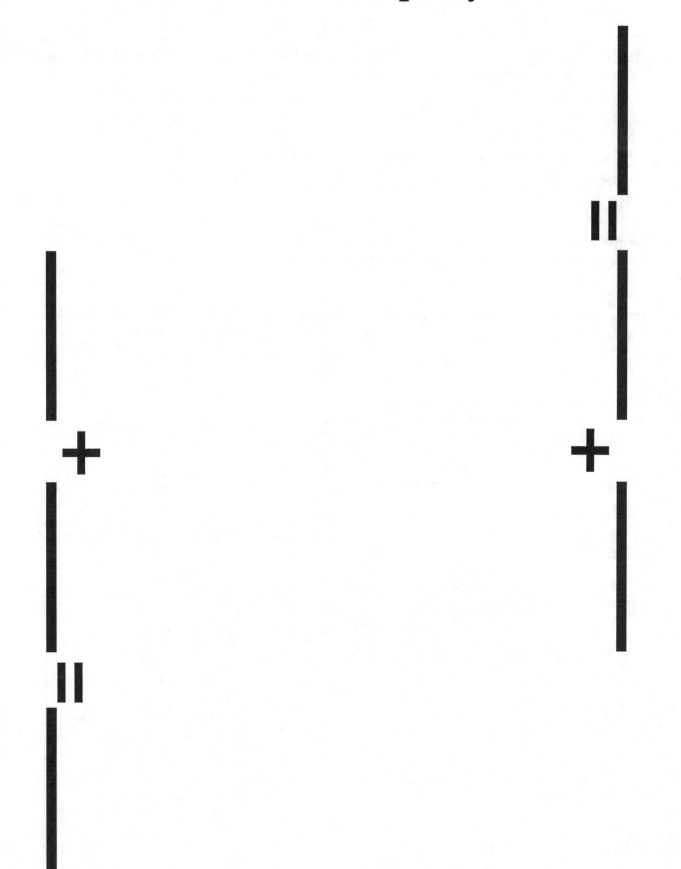

Float or Sink

Purpose
Using a set of objects and a tub of water, children will experiment and discover what floats or sinks.

Materials
- A deep tub
- Access to water and a sink
- A set of items that float and sink on a tray
- Optional recording sheet (page 340)

Preparation
Take the tub to the sink. Fill it to the line with water approximately 3 inches deep. Carefully take the water tub to the table.

Instructions
Children should study the objects on the tray. Have them take one item from the tray at a time and guess if the object will float or sink. Have them drop the item into the water tub and decide if they made the correct conclusion about the item. Follow the same procedure for all objects on the tray. Children may then fill out the worksheet with answers.

Clean-Up
Lay all items on the tray. Walk the tub to the sink and dump out water. Dry hands and any water that spilled on the table. Children leave tub on the table, and return to their seats.

Helpful Hints
The following items could be used at this center: cork, piece of wood, glass bottle with a cork, small bar of soap, bone, straw, small plastic container, cork, styrofoam cup, small ball, sponge, shell, nail, and some coins.

Float or Sink?

Circle those items that float. Put an X on those items that sink.

Summertime Sunglasses

Purpose

Children will make a pair of sunglasses. Students will learn the purpose of wearing sunglasses to protect their eyes from harmful rays, and understand it is also harmful to their eyes to look directly at the sun.

Materials

- Sunglass Patterns (pages 342-343)
- Oaktag
- Green, blue, and yellow cellophane, pre-cut to fit glasses
- Crayons
- Scissors
- Tape or glue

Preparation

Reproduce patterns onto oaktag. Cut out the lenses. Precut cellophane a little bigger then the lenses so children can attach it to the inside of the glasses.

Instructions

Have children select a pattern for a pair of sunglasses. Color and cut them out. Paste cellophane into the holes of the glasses. Have them attach the earpieces. They may use the decorations on the glasses.

Clean-Up

Close glue and make sure none gets onto the cellophane.

Sunglasses Patterns

Sunglasses Patterns *(cont.)*

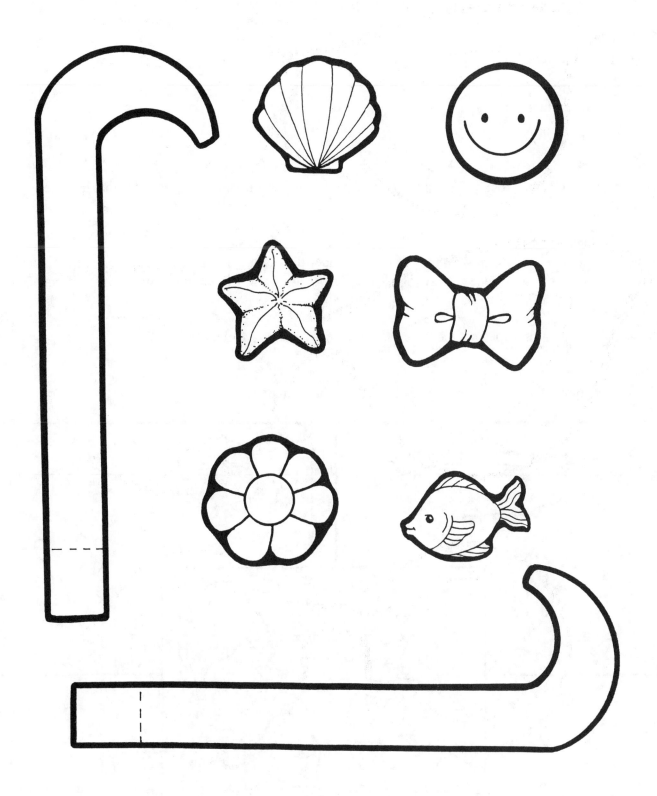

Water Color Wash

Purpose

Children will use fluorescent crayons to create an underwater scene complete with fish, seaweed, and other ocean dwellers. Apply a coat of thinned, blue tempera paint atop the entire scene.

Materials

- Fluorescent crayons
- Drawing paper
- Blue tempera paint
- Wide paint brushes

Preparation

Have supplies ready for children, including wide paint brushes and blue tempera paint that has been thinned.

Instructions

Allow students to brainstorm what they might see under the ocean. Then, using the fluorescent crayons draw their scenes onto a piece of drawing paper. Using blue paint will create an underwater effect.

Clean Up

Make sure all paint is wiped off the tables and, all paint brushes are cleaned.

Helpful Hints

Students may use the patterns on page 345 to add to their underwater scenes.

Underwater Patterns

Advice Story

Purpose
Students will write a story advising students who will enter the class next year what to expect.

Materials
- Story form (page 347)
- Pencils

Preparation
Reproduce the story for each student. Students can simply fill in the blanks or they may write their stories onto paper.

Instructions
Children should decide what information they want to include about this school year. They should then write a story about their year in the classroom. The story can then be shared with the class or with students in incoming classes.

Clean-Up
Make sure papers are picked up and stacked neatly, and that pencils are sharpened and ready to use.

Story

_____
(Date)

Hello!

My name is _____ and I have been in
_____ class. I want to tell you
(teacher's name and grade)
about some of the fun things we did. Some of them were

_____

_____

_____

_____

My favorite thing was_____ .

I hope you learn as much and have as much fun as I did this year in

_____.
(grade)

Water Safety

Purpose

Children will better understand that there are rules for making water-play safe and fun.

Materials

- Water safety poster for center (pages 350-351)
- Student copy of poster (page 349)
- Crayons

Preparation

Reproduce the water safety poster for the center. Color it and display it at the center. Reproduce copies for the children to copy.

Instructions

Children should read the rules on the poster and decide what determines a safety rule. They may want to add a rule of their own. Then, they may color the little poster.

Clean-Up

Put all supplies away.

Student Water Safety Poster

Water safety rules

1. Never swim alone.

2. Play in or near the water only if there is supervision.

3. Learn the safety rules of any place where you play in or near water. Always obey these rules.

4. Listen to the lifeguard.

5. If playing by the **ocean**, ask the lifeguard about the tides and undertows.

Water Safety Teacher Poster

Water Safety Rules

1. Never swim alone.

2. Play in or near the water only if there is supervision.

3. Learn the safety rules of any place where you play in or near water. Always obey these rules.

4. Listen to the lifeguard.

5. If playing by the ocean, ask the lifeguard about the tides and undertows.

Summer Vacation Stories

Purpose

Children create stories about what they will do during summer vacation, or write stories about something they would like to do.

Materials

- Writing paper
- Pens and pencils
- Vacation paper (page 354)
- Cover (page 353)
- Crayons

Preparation

Reproduce the shape paper for children to write on. Reproduce covers for children to color.

Instructions

Ask children what they plan to do during the summer. Have them write about their summer vacation on the shape paper. When they're done, they can color the cover and add their title and name.

Clean-Up

Separate covers and paper into two different stacks for children to use.

Vacation Stories Book Cover

Vacation Shape Paper

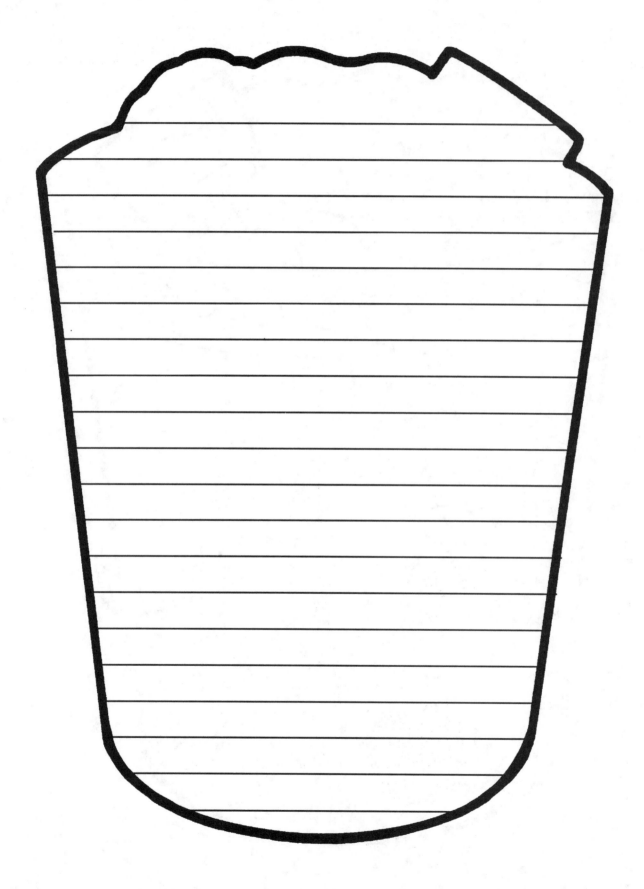

Sand Tub

Purpose

The purpose of this learning center is to provide an alternate way to practice writing letters, words, and numerals. By writing on the bottom of this tub, the children can actually feel and see the formation of each letter and numeral.

Materials

- Deep plastic tub with a flat bottom
- Sand

Preparation

Cover the bottom of the tub with approximately one inch/2.5 cm of sand.

Instructions

Using the index finger on their writing hand, children practice printing the upper and lower case letters of the alphabet. They will also write the numerals 0-9. It works best to smooth out the sand evenly and then form the letter or numeral.

Clean-Up

It works best to allow the child working at the sand tub to sit on the floor. Remind the students to keep the sand inside the tub. When children are finished at this center, they should wash their hands and return the tub to the appropriate place.

Helpful Hints

As a follow-up to the sand tub center, the teacher might want to have students trace letters and numerals with their fingers on sandpaper. This will reinforce the correct formation letters and numerals. Children might also benefit from writing words and math problems in the sand.

Introduction

This section is intended to help you manage your centers. The following information will make setting up, identifying, scheduling your centers a snap. These pages are ready for you to reproduce, color, and laminate if you wish.

Table of Contents for Classroom Management

Center Schedules

There are many ways of scheduling children at centers.

One way is to use library pockets and craft sticks. On each library pocket write the name of the center. Attach the library pockets to a large poster board. On a craft stick write each child's name. Slip the sticks with the children's names that are to work at that particular center into the library pocket. Children can then read their own names and go to the appropriate center.

Using a wheel is another way to schedule children into centers. Make your own wheel or use the one on page 358. Write the name of the center in each section. Using a paper fastener attach the wheel onto a large chart with the children's name and turn the chart to the children's names.

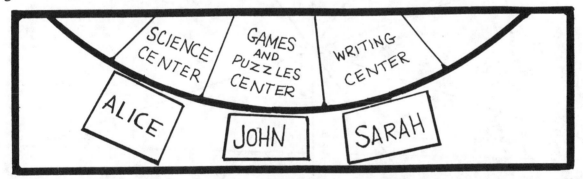

Another easy way to manage the centers is to post a chart listing the available centers in the classroom. This can be written on tagboard. Print each child's name on a clothespin. The clothespins can then be clipped to the name of the center where the student is to work. These clips can be moved each day to the next center by the student or teacher. This chart will help the teacher keep track of who has completed each center. Ideally you won't have more than two students at a center.

Center Schedules *(cont.)*

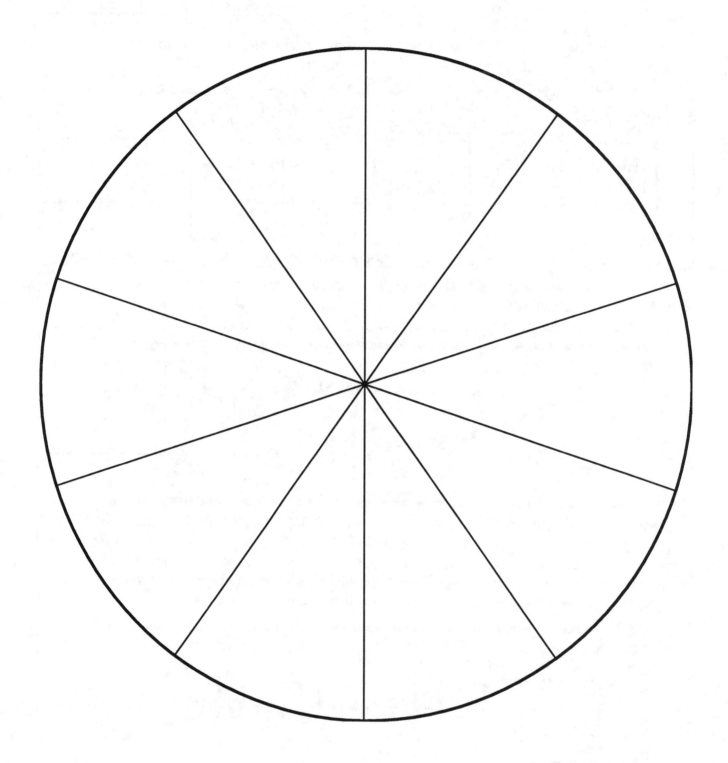

Center Recording Sheet

Write the name of each center as you work on it. The teacher will mark the marked square when you have completed the center. Attach this sheet to a folder or packet.

| **Name:** |
| **Date:** |
| **Center Completed:** |
| 1. |
| 2. |
| 3. |
| 4. |
| 5. |
| 6. |
| 7. |
| 8. |
| 9. |
| 10. |

Supply Request Letter

Dear Parents,

Can you help us with supplies for our centers? If so, please send:

_____

_____

_____

_____

Thank you!

Supply Request Letter

Dear Parents,

Our class will be working at many fun centers this month. Many of our activities will require items you may already have at home. Would you please take a minute and see if you have any of the following items on hand? If so, please send them in with your child.

_____

_____

_____

_____

Thank you!

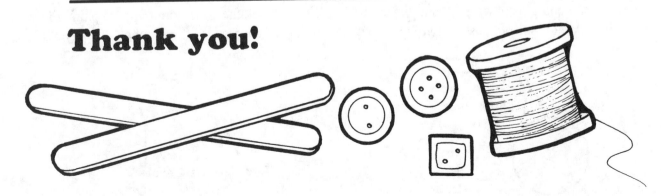

Center Signs

To help identify your centers, reproduce the signs on the following pages, color them, and hang them at the appropriate center. You might choose to reproduce them onto index paper and color them in with crayons or color pencils. Laminate them for durability.

They may be used at the centers in a variety of ways.

- Tape them to the wall.

- Punch two holes on either side of the sign and run yarn or wire through the holes. Hang the yarn over a nail or hook.

- Punch a hole and put it over a nail.

- Make a clothespin stand. Cut a tennis ball in half with a craft knife or scissors. Line both halves with plastic wrap. Fill halves with plaster of Paris. Place one paper towel roll tube into each ball, pressing gently so that the tube remains straight; allow plaster to dry thoroughly. Peel away tennis ball and plastic wrap. Paint plaster, tube and the two clothespins with tempera paint; allow to dry. Attach one clothespin holding the sign to the top of each paper towel tube. Display at the center.

362

Reading Center

Seasonal

Special

Center

Drama and Stories Center

Hands-On Center

This Center is Open

374

Directions for Students

Some form of symbolic directions for students will make the centers easier to use even if you orally explain a center. These symbols will be especially helpful for those who aren't yet reading.

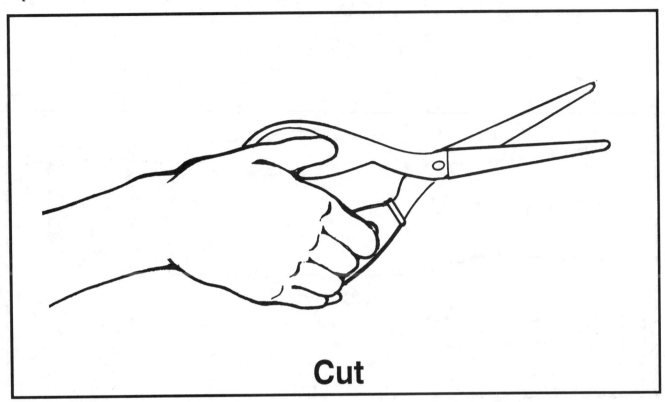

Cut

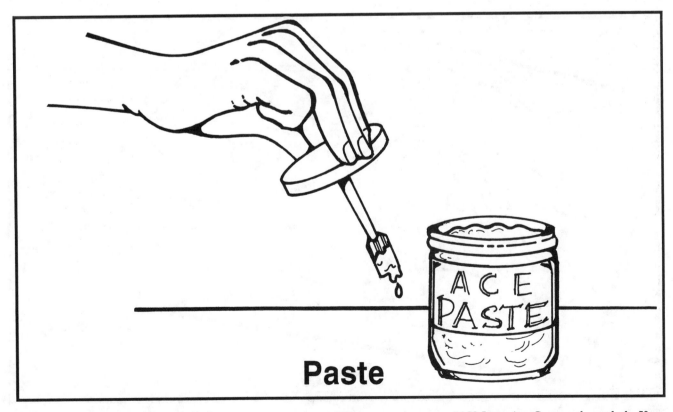

Paste

Directions for Students *(cont.)*

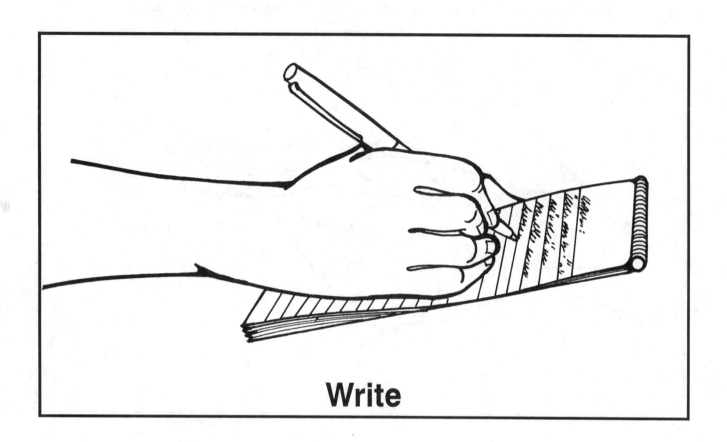

Write

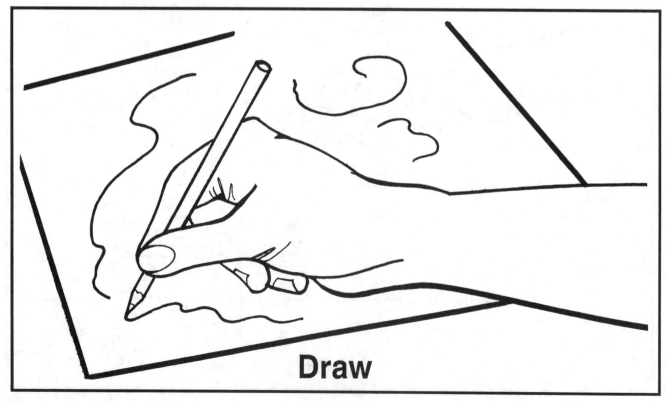

Draw

Directions for Students *(cont.)*

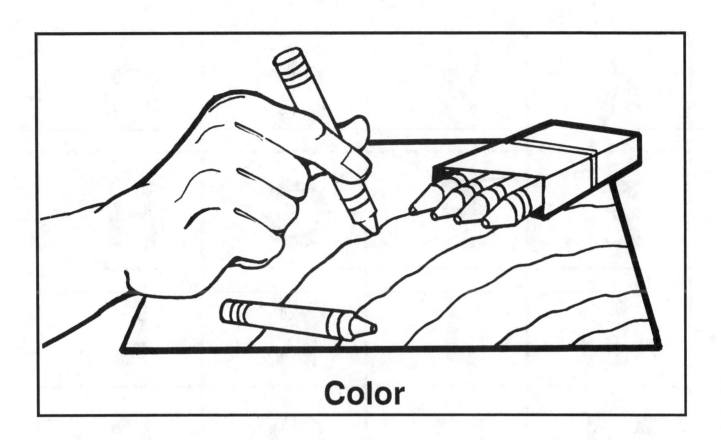

Color

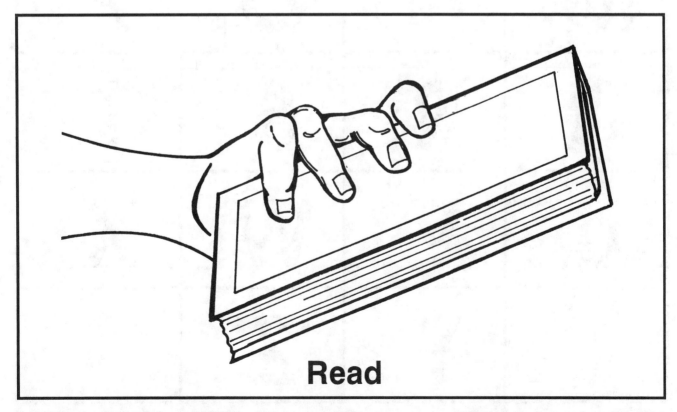

Read

Alphabet

Upper Case

A	B	C	D
E	F	G	H
I	J	K	L
M	N	O	P
Q	R	S	T
U	V	W	X
	Y	Z	

378

Alphabet

Lower Case

a	b	c	d
e	f	g	h
i	j	k	l
m	n	o	p
q	r	s	t
u	v	w	x
	y	z	

Numbers

0-10

0	1	2
3	4	5
6	7	8
9	10	

Story Paper

Name _____

Story Paper

Name _____

Story Paper

Name _____

Bibliography

Teacher Resources

Charles, C. M. *Individualizing Instruction.* The C. V. Mosby Company, 1980

Darrow, Helen Fisher, & Van Allen, R. *Independent Activities For Creative Learning.* Columbia University, 1961

Decker, Celia Anita, & John R. Decker. *Planning and Administrating Early Childhood Programs.* Charles E. Merrill, 1984

Evertson, Carolyn M., et al. *Organizing and Managing the Elementary School Classroom.* The University of Texas at Austin: The Research and Development Center for Teacher Education, 1979

Fennema, E. *Manipulatives in the Classroom. The Arithmetic Teacher,* pages 350-352, 1973

Glasser, Joyce Fern. *The Elementary School: Learning Center for Independent Study.* Parker, 1971

Individualized Instruction: *Every Child a Winner.* John Wiley and Sons, Inc.

Ingram, Barbara, Nancy Jones, Marlene LeButt. *The Workshop Approach to Classroom Interest Centers: A Teacher Handbook of Learning Games And Activities.* Parker, 1975

Kaplan, Sandra N., Kaplan, JoAnn B., Madsen, Shelia K., & Taylor, Bette K. *Change for Children: Ideas and Activities for Individualizing Learning.* Goodyear, 1973

Kinghorn, Harriet. *Classroom and Workshop Tested Games, Puzzles, and Activities for the Elementary School.* Parker, 1975

Individualized Instruction: *Every Child a Winner.* John Wiley and Sons, Inc.

Rapport, Virginia. *Learning Centers: Children on Their Own.* Association for Childhood Education International, 1970

Stephens, Karen. *Preschool and Primary Learning Centers.* Pages 44-45.

Children's Books

Aliki. *The Story of Johnny Appleseed.* Prentice, 1963

Borden, Louise. *Caps, Hats, Socks, and Mittens.* Scholastic, 1989

Cole, Joanna. *The Magic School Bus: Lost in the Solar System.* Scholastic, 1990

dePaola, Tomie selected and illustrated by. *Tomie De Paola's Mother Goose.* Putnam, 1986

Galdone, Paul illustrated by. *Jack and the Beanstalk.* Clarion, 1982

Howe, John retold by. *Jack and the Beanstalk. Vol. 1.* Little, 1989

Kellogg, Steven. *Johnny Appleseed.* Morrow, 1988.

Kellogg, Steven. *The Mystery of the Missing Red Mitten.* Dial, 1974

Potter, Beatrix. *Tale of Peter Rabbit.* Warne, 1987.

Williams, Margery. *The Velveteen Rabbit.* Doubleday, 1922; 1992